BACKWARD GLANCES: FAITH THROUGH A REARVIEW MIRROR

STEVE & ANNE WEIHSMANN

Copyright © 2011 by Steve and Anne Weihsmann

Backward Glances: Faith Through a Rearview Mirror
by Steve and Anne Weihsmann

Printed in the United States of America

ISBN 9781619044418

All rights reserved solely by the author. The author guarantees all contents are original and do not infringe upon the legal rights of any other person or work. No part of this book may be reproduced in any form without the permission of the author. The views expressed in this book are not necessarily those of the publisher.

Unless otherwise indicated, Bible quotations are taken from The Holy Bible, **New International Version (NIV).** Copyright © 1973, 1978, 1984 by International Bible Society. Used by permission of Zondervan Bible Publishers.

www.xulonpress.com

PREFACE

Trying to write the preface together proved to be more difficult than writing, editing and compiling a book of eighty-three essays. Steve and I made several approaches and could not bring the preface in for a smooth landing. We began to realize that writing this part together was a blind approach through the fog of proper names and pronouns. Since Steve's essays fill the majority of our book, we decided that I would write the preface and guide you onto the runway of thoughts, ideas, challenges and encouragements found in our individual essays.

I have been a dedicated journal writer since my college days, and have also experienced both the hard, decidedly unglamorous work and intense satisfaction of seeing editorials, short stories and a novel in print. It is rare for me to go one day without writing something: notes or letters, a phrase for a future essay, a favorite quote or a journal entry. The pure written word holds power and joy for me; I love the fact that Jesus called Himself the WORD.

Steve writes letters and editorials, keeps a prayer and study journal and composes essays. For the past several years his essays have appeared in our church newsletter and in the monthly faith column of two local newspapers. After hearing positive comments from people around town about the earthiness and "man slant" of his essays, a book seemed like a good way to preserve them. We have included a few of my original writings, and thus our book has touched down in your life.

Steve and I have been spouses for thirty-one years, parents for twenty-nine, and a clergy couple for twenty-seven. Each role has woven threads of color and contrast into our lives. Ruth Graham once said of her marriage to famous evangelist Billy Graham, "We are happily incompatible." I do not remember how many years of sweat equity Steve and I poured into our marriage before finding that simple quote and giving ourselves the freedom to celebrate our differences, which in turn makes our commonalities sweeter. Encompassing all of the differences are two non-negotiables: Our love for our two sons, two daughters and son-in-law, and the journey of faith we walk together.

There is nearsightedness, farsightedness, and hind-sightedness. This book is about the last—looking back at our experiences through the lenses of marriage, parenting and professional ministry to capture some of God's truth found in people, nature, the laws of physics, grief, cars, deer-hunting, computers, roofing, fishing, electricity, the courtroom and even Mr. Potato Head.

We have not achieved perfect hind-sight. Sometimes we let our rearview mirrors get so coated with the grime of our present circumstances that we cannot see how God has faithfully navigated us around the potholes and over the crumbled pavement of our past. Sometimes we ignore the mirror's image, oblivious to the danger that may be swallowing the distance between us. And sometimes our mirrors are in need of repair or replacement, cracked by unavoidable collisions with immovable ideas.

Thank you, Gethsemane Covenant Church family, for granting Steve a six-week sabbatical, giving him time and space to edit his essays and prepare our book together. It was a sweet time in our marriage. We continue to believe in a God of Hope, Healing and Peace, such as we have seen work among you.

Anne Weihsmann
October, 2011

PART I

THROUGH STEVE'S REARVIEW MIRROR

A DISTURBING FIND

An article in the *Duluth News-Tribune* was reprinted from an article by Jeffrey Weiss of the *Dallas Morning News*. The article was entitled, "Poll suggests most Americans tolerant of faith differences."

The poll to which Weiss referred was a survey done by the Pew Forum on Religion and Public Life. The sample size (the number of people interviewed) was very large—36,000 people, which makes the results very reliable. One question that was asked was, "Can many religions lead to eternal life?" And 70% of religious Americans said "Yes."

We might expect such an answer from some of the religious groups interviewed—American Hindus, Buddhists and others who are religiously tolerant. It is a mark of some faith traditions that religions nestle nicely inside each other or peacefully co-exist. And in American religion it has become politically incorrect to claim knowledge of absolute truth. It is ironic that politics have come to dominate faith, especially in light of our nation being founded to ensure freedom to worship apart from political pressures. The disturbing find is that 79% of American Catholics, 72% of American Orthodox Christians and 66% of American Protestants also said "Yes, many religions lead to eternal life."

What this means is that many American "Christians" have lost touch with the Bible and with the truth of the Gospel. One of the simplest, most straight forward statements of the Gospel is found in 1 John 5:11-13: "And this is the testimony: God has given us eternal life, and this life is in His Son. He who has the Son has life; he who does not have the Son of God does not have life. I write these things to you who believe in the name of the Son of God so that you may know that you have eternal life."

I believe that God is fair in all things and makes allowances for people who have never heard the name of His Son, but who worship Him in Spirit and in truth nonetheless. C.S. Lewis describes such a case in "The Last Battle," one of *The Chronicles of Narnia.*

That being said, why do so many American "Christians" who have access to the Bible not believe what it says? I think there are three main reasons:

1. People have a Bible but do not read it; they do not know what it says.
2. People do not consider the Bible to be authoritative.
3. People re-interpret plain statements to mean things not intended by the Biblical writers, but which fit the way they wish to live.

Faithful Christians have always been people of the Book, reading it and studying it, allowing it to be their manual for living and choosing it as the authority to which they appeal when there is a question to be answered. Though the Bible does not deal with every matter, there are principles that can be applied. Faithful Christians try not to twist or do violence to the Bible or to its principles.

I wonder what the future of the Bible will be in American society and in Christian society. Centuries ago, before the invention of the printing press, there were few Bibles, only those that could be copied by hand and purchased by those with means. People depended upon hearing the word of God from priests and pastors and upon the Bible stories reflected in the artwork of stained glass windows. With the advent of printing, Bibles became common and affordable. Now we have Bibles in print, on CD, on computers, even on I-phones. But do we use what we have? Do we know what the Bible says? Do we believe what it says? Do we care?

A person who does not stay in touch with the truth loses the ability to discern it. Apparently, many Americans, even "Christians" already have.

A FAULTY CIRCUIT BREAKER

The dryer quit working, which was probably okay because it was an old dryer. It came to us second hand and served us quite a few years. The heating element went out just before vacation and when we got back the weather was nice enough to hang clothes outside, so we did that. Some friends at church heard of our need and offered a dryer which they were replacing with a new one.

Our house is not normal. The people who live there are not normal either, but it is the house itself that posed a problem when the dryer went out. The washer and dryer are in the upstairs bathroom, which is very convenient. But the hallway to the bathroom is too narrow to get an appliance into it, which is not so convenient. We have to rent a special materials lift to get appliances onto the back deck, and then in through the deck door and then through the bathroom door frame, minus the door, to make it work.

We did that. And hooked up the dryer we had been given, set the cycle and pushed the button. At the moment when there should have been a nice humming sound, there was silence. We scratched our heads. Then we checked the power cord, took the dryer apart and examined all the electrical connections, gave it menacing looks and prayed over it. Finally we called our friend, Gordy, for help.

"Do you have one of those testers?" he asked. "The kind with a black and a red wire, each connected to a metal pin, and a light bulb in between?" I did. "Touch one pin to a wire and the other to a ground and see if you have electricity flowing," suggested Gordy. I did that and I didn't die. So I continued testing—first the dryer, then the power cord, then the wall outlet, and lastly the circuit breaker. It is rare that a circuit breaker is faulty, but this one was. It was just loose enough that electricity had made an arc and burned one of the bus bars. I turned the power off, took out the bad breaker and replaced it with a new one, locating the new one in an unused spot so as not to repeat the problem.

It made me think: sometimes human beings have faulty circuit breakers. They have things in their lives that arc and burn and interrupt power for living. Things that make them scratch their heads, things that remain hidden until some kind of tester is applied.

God is good about applying a tester. Sometimes He uses the Bible, sometimes a friend, sometimes His Holy Spirit, sometimes common sense. The result is that we locate the thing that is not right. Israel's King David wrote in Psalm 69, "You know my folly, O God; my guilt is not hidden from You." God's purpose in helping us discover our sin is that we will want it out, like the faulty circuit breaker, so it cannot harm us anymore. A bad circuit breaker, left in, can start a fire that burns a house down. And sin, not addressed, can burn a life down.

We often leave things as they are, because we think we can control the consequences of our actions, of our sin. But we can't completely control the consequences.

How many times have we said, "I didn't expect that to happen!" when something we were doing went wrong?

Electrically and spiritually, we need three things: to get the faulty things out, to get the new and good things in, and to keep the power connected.

A HAND ON THE FISH

When he hooked it, he knew it was huge. And with only six pound test line, it was going to take some finesse to get it to the boat. He let it run and then carefully reeled it in. Repeatedly it swam for cover and he let it go, then he brought it back slowly. When he got it next to the boat, he could see how large it was. He didn't have a net that was big enough to properly handle the great northern, so he resorted to an old fisherman's trick. Hanging on to his pole with one hand, he gently put his other hand in the water and stroked the fish. Immediately it took off and he let it pull on the drag a while. Then he cranked it back and tried petting the fish again. Several more times it zipped away from the boat, but each time the distance was shorter, until finally, tired out, the fish stayed by the boat and didn't recoil at the fisherman's touch.

It wasn't easy to get the fish into the boat. He didn't want to hurt the fish, just to measure it. But without a net, getting it into the boat was a problem, even if it was tired and compliant. Once he lost his balance and almost lost the fish. But with perseverance and an unhurried manner, gained from years of mechanical work in awkward positions and tight places, he managed to get one hand around the jawbone, near the mouth and away from the sharp teeth. The jawbone was as smooth as the inside of a seashell. He avoided the gills so the northern could breathe easily. Knowing that when the fish left the water it would fight and flop, he thought through the maneuver he would use. In one deft motion he lifted the fish over the boat, dropped his pole and took hold of the other jawbone. The fish was landed, and not a moment too soon, for the hook had come free and the fish might have escaped if his grip on the jawbone had slipped.

He couldn't be sure, but it looked like the biggest northern he had ever caught. He laid it in the bottom of the boat and, holding it in place, made pencil marks on the hull at the nose and tip of the tail. Then, as carefully as before, he scooped the fish up in his workman's hands and lowered it into the lake. He held onto it for several minutes, pushing it away and pulling it back, to get oxygen into the gills. He could feel the fish recovering, and when it was sufficiently refreshed, he squeezed the tail once and watched it dive for the bottom. He knew the fish was happy to be alive. And he was happy to have let it go, even after he found out that it *was* the largest northern he had ever caught, measuring forty-three-and-a-half inches. He told me the name of the lake, but fishermen guard their secrets closely and I cannot reveal it, except to say it is in Canada and you reach it by plane.

If it had been me, I think I would have kept that fish and maybe had it mounted. But hearing how it was let go gave me something to think about. It put me in mind of how God deals with us. He wants us to know and trust Him, and so He does everything He can to reel us in to Himself. But He is not interested in trophies. He is interested in friends and so He handles us carefully and kindly. His purpose in bringing us to Himself is to make sure we have a chance at really living. It might be said that His hand can gently lift us from the lake of poor decisions into the healing waters of abundant life.

He doesn't destroy us if we choose not to respond to Him. Even then He continues to let us enjoy this life and the beauty that is everywhere in the world. At the edge of eternity some find that they have destroyed themselves by rejecting Him. But He continues to catch and release us until He knows one more time won't make any difference. He lets us choose whether or not to stay in His boat.

A fish has no way of knowing whether the fisherman's hand on it is kind or not. But we can know about God's hand on us. His hand promises forgiveness. His hand is the one that sets us free from every kind of captivity. In the person of Jesus, His hand bears the print of a nail to let us know what He was willing to suffer in order to have us become His friends. Jesus said, "I have come that they may have life, and have it to the full" (John 10:10). In this world there is real love and there is something that passes for it. In His hand is the real love.

A LITTLE AFTER MIDNIGHT

It was a little after midnight when the fire broke out. Twenty-eight men and two women from four departments valiantly battled the flames. Twice they were inside the storeroom off the bedroom where the woman was trapped. Twice the heat was too intense. When the staircase burned through and the bedroom floor felt spongy, they laddered the house front and back.

The ladder truck had pulled in first. Behind it was the pumper. Behind that was a tanker and behind the tanker was a square vinyl pool three feet deep. A large hose with a rectangular mouth sucked water like a vacuum and sent it up the line to the pumper. From there half a dozen smaller hoses snaked to the burning home. The dirt around the trucks soon turned to mud as runoff from the hoses drained back toward a small pond.

While stars shone overhead in a pitch-black sky, a halogen light on the ladder truck cut through the furious billows of smoke. Axes, chain-saws and pike poles were hoisted onto the roof. Foam was added to the water spray. It was chilly for August, surprisingly cold just fifty feet from the inferno.

In a steady stream, as their air supply alarms sounded, firefighters kept coming from the blaze to the trucks. They rested briefly, drank Gatorade, splashed water on their faces and cleaned their visors. As they lifted their helmets and peeled off their masks, steam rose from their heads. On their knees or on all fours, on a blue weave tarp, they waited patiently while colleagues unfastened the spent forty-five-minute bottles and snapped fresh ones into the steel ring on their backpacks. Their faces were grim, but confident. They knew what they were doing. A few gulped air as they were assisted toward the tarp, giving evidence of their determination to stay in the house just a little bit longer, and not to let the fire win.

At four o'clock the Red Cross came with handmade quilts and soft drinks, hugs, tears, hope and realism.

At five o'clock a tawny cat slipped out onto the first story roof through a gash made in the second story wall by an axe. It disappeared into another gash, ripped into the roof by a chain-saw. The sky was beginning to lighten.

At six o'clock a uniformed woman police officer, a friend of the family members who had rushed to the scene, confirmed the dreaded expectation: the woman had perished. Her body had been found.

The sun was now fully up, shooting golden rays against blue violet morning glories climbing a white trellis. The house was smoldering. The roof had fallen in. The second floor had collapsed onto the first floor. Ruby-throated humming birds, stunned by the overnight change yet determined to find their accustomed nectar, buzzed to two feeders hanging over the front door. As I looked to the left I saw a black bear, carved from a tree trunk and standing in a flowerbed. It held a sign that said, "Welcome."

The investigation suggested it was an oscillating pedestal fan that caused the fire. But why it happened will never be known this side of heaven.

In the face of such unspeakable tragedy, can we trust in a God of grace, love, peace and kindness? The woman who perished would say, "Yes." Her husband, who escaped the fire but suffered burns to his head and arms while trying to rescue her, says, "Yes." The woman's life continues with God, because she trusted in Him. She has new life, secure against all injury for all eternity. But how do we know this?

Jesus once had a conversation with a woman whose brother had just tragically died. She was disappointed that Jesus had not prevented the brother from dying and she told Him so. Jesus said to her, "I am the resurrection and the life; he who believes in Me will never die. Do you believe this?" She replied to Him, "Yes, Lord; I believe that You are the Christ, the Son of God, even He who was to come into the world" (John 11:27).

The brother had been dead four days. Still, Jesus went over to the tomb and called in a loud voice for him to come out. He came out—alive.

Jesus, out of love for His friend, raised him from the dead with witnesses around. That is how we know we can trust Him to give life. He gives it even to those who die. It is not all over a little after our own midnight.

This article was prepared with help from Mr. David Ankarlo (the husband of Patricia, the woman who perished) and from Hermantown, Minnesota Fire Chief Ron Minter.

AN ANSWER FOR THE ATHEIST

In his book *Cries of the Heart*, Christian apologist Ravi Zacharias makes an interesting observation. When he talks with atheists (who say there is no God), the conversation invariably comes around to the problem of evil in the world. Atheists wonder how there can be a good God when there is so much that is evil all about us. While the problem of evil is not simple, the very question gives hope to a searching atheist.

Consider this line of thought. To characterize something as "evil" implies that there is something else which can be characterized as "good." Most atheists will agree to this. If there is "good," then it follows that there is some kind of standard for saying so. We might call it moral law. Most atheists will agree to this also.

The next logical step is to suggest that if there is a moral law, there must be a moral law giver. The Christian takes this step and says the moral law giver is God. The atheist is usually reluctant to go in the same direction. The atheist might posit no moral law at all, espousing random chance in the universe, but if so, then there are no good or bad events, just neutral events. A person dying at the hands of a murderer is in the same category as drinking a cup of coffee.

Most atheists are not completely neutral in regard to human events, so they must at least consider what they use as a standard for moral law instead of God. It may be the individual, but there are problems with individuals. Most atheists recognize that individuals are flawed. Alternatively, the atheist may turn to society as the standard—the idea that together we are better than any one of us. But that is not totally satisfactory either. Different societies have different and competing values. As Zacharias points out, some societies want to love their neighbors while others wish to eat them. Which has the correct moral law?

Many atheists acknowledge that there is a standard to which humanity aspires, a perfection that is desired, but not reached, even if they cannot name it. Curiously this comes close to the Christian concept of God, Who is a perfect standard by virtue of His character. Atheists are uncomfortable with God as the standard even though He fits the definition, suggesting that the pages of Scripture make Him seem less than perfect when He punishes sin. But most atheists have a sense of fairness, and want sin to be punished when it is against them. Punishment of criminal activity is just as important to atheists as to anyone else. All people seek justice.

The sticking point may be in how we identify sin. For the Christian, everything is measured against God's character, which does not change. The atheist must use a moveable boundary, adjustable according to current thought, practice and "whatever the market will bear." Usually, the market will bear quite a lot in the interest of preserving personal freedom, and sometimes personal freedom is valued even more than moral goodness. Atheists, who tend to acknowledge the physical world and dismiss the spiritual one, look to see if any physical harm comes from free human action. If not, then even questionable morals seem all right. Christians will allow that there are invisible injuries to consider, which may wound emotions and souls, not just bodies.

Atheists sometimes object to God as the moral law giver because they think He impinges on personal freedom. According to their understanding of the Bible, God says, "Believe or else..." But society as law giver does essentially the same thing, saying "Behave or else..." The record of Scripture is that God does not curtail personal freedom, but gives an immense amount of it, for the common good, starting in Genesis with the injunction to Adam and Eve to refrain from the fruit of only one tree in a large garden of trees. Disbelief in God does not bring His punishment so much as it brings natural consequences, which God Himself hopes we will not have to experience.

Which brings us to a final question: if there is a moral law in the universe, and if it is God, and if He grants great personal freedom, why does He not prevent all or most tragedy and atrocity? Again, the answer is not simple, but ultimately it has to do with God's ability to bring good out of the bad things that happen, to redeem what people ruin. It also has to do with God's ability to make up for the worst that can happen by granting life after death. Atheists typically do not accept that life may continue after death. But if life does continue (and Jesus' resurrection is evidence that it does), evil can never have the last word. God can apply justice to an evil-doer after death. God can also apply mercy to victims of evil after death. In eternity the "sting of death," as the Apostle Paul called it, bites those who have harmed others, but is removed for those who have trusted in a good God.

The existence of evil in the world does not disprove the existence of God. The more likely conclusion is that both individuals, and society as a whole, are flawed, and that the world does not live by a good standard. God and Christianity offer hope in the quest for a good standard, even for the atheist—perhaps especially for the atheist.

BULL MOOSE

I was driving to Virginia, Minnesota, on the Iron Range, and I had just passed Cotton when the moose exited a snow covered path. What I saw was chestnut-colored, shaggy and huge. He still wore his rack, which was impressive. He was not in a hurry, but was traveling with purpose and crossed in front of me on Route 53, slowing to look in my direction as he gained the shoulder. I pushed the flasher button on top of the steering column, eased off the gas and drifted into the other lane of the double lane highway to give him more room. I had heard stories about these animals being unpredictable and unafraid of cars. There was no need to worry though. He kept going, obviously more intent on his destination than on an iron thing intersecting his route. It was the first time I had seen a bull moose.

I know there are stretches of road, like the Gunflint Trail, where moose are more common. They are seen regularly as they venture out onto the ice-encrusted asphalt to eat salt laid down by snowplows. But it was a rare sighting for me. Had I passed that spot twenty seconds earlier or twenty seconds later I would have missed him altogether. So it was a privilege and a thrill.

The moose sighting came in the middle of a prayer I was praying as I drove to a meeting with my accountability group. I was praying for the grandson of a couple in our church. Gabe, just seven years old, had been battling cancer. I was wondering, as I was praying, how likely it might be that God would do a miracle. Gabe had already been through chemo and, after a brief exploratory, was rejected as a candidate for surgery to remove the cancer. The cancer broke off into "seeds" that went everywhere in his abdomen. But another doctor suggested a relatively new procedure—a stem cell transplant from one of Gabe's parents—to stimulate the growth of healthy cells in Gabe's body. The second doctor was willing to try the surgery and then do the stem cell transplant.

God has not often spoken so directly to me in prayer, but on that day there was a clear message: "The crisis is past."

The surgery took place and it went well. Gabe was, for the moment, cancer free, and the stem cell transplant came up the next month. Though tender in age, Gabe had a mature faith. He knew that there are tragedies in life and events we cannot explain well, but he said to his folks, "If there wasn't a God, who would perform the miracles?" He believed, and I believed, he was in the middle of a miracle.

For most of us, miracles are rare occurrences, although I'm not sure they have to be. The Bible is full of them. Faith is all about trusting what you believe to be true without necessarily seeing the object of faith at that moment. Had I not seen the bull moose, I would still have believed such creatures exist. There are pictures, there are eyewitness accounts and there are stories enough to be sure about that. But it was nice to see a bull moose for myself. I was reminded that just because a thing is rare, doesn't mean it should be discounted. God lets us see rare things to fuel our faith.

Thomas, doubting that Jesus could live again after being crucified, determined not to believe what he had heard unless he could put a finger in the nail print of Jesus' hand and put his hand in the spear wound in Jesus' side. Jesus appeared to Thomas and gave that opportunity, telling him, "Stop doubting and believe." The rare thing Thomas needed was provided and Thomas stopped doubting and believed (John 20:24-31).

God is not a genie whose lamp we rub for miracles. He is not at our beck and call. But He does seem willing to provide what we most need when we most need it, even something that occurs only rarely, so that we may obtain the salvation of our souls and have the assurance of His help for daily living.

CAN PEOPLE OF FAITH AND PEOPLE OF SCIENCE TALK WITH EACH OTHER?

I participated in an on-line chat room discussion covering various aspects of faith and science. The conversation ranged over topics such as evolution, archaeology, the fossil record, the biblical narrative, court cases involving the teaching of creation in public schools, soft tissue in dinosaur bones, carbon and potassium-argon dating, intelligent design, irreducible complexity and the reliability of sources. It was a fascinating conversation. It was surprising too, as I discovered that there is a wide spectrum of thought and interpretation of the data available to us. For example, on the faith side of the discussion, in addition to young earth creationists, there are also old earth creationists, and there are some Christians who hold that evolution is God's creative mechanism. And on the science side of the discussion, there are evolutionary scientists who do not think the fossil record supports change from one species into another. I am still trying to absorb the various viewpoints and to check what I learned to see what is valid and what is not.

It is sometimes difficult for people of faith and people of science to talk with each other because there are suspicions on both sides. People of faith are concerned that the science folks are determined to erase God from the universe, and the science folks wonder if the people of faith have checked their brains at the door of the Church. Neither of these things is necessarily true, although both have been true on occasion. Can there be a meaningful dialogue between the two groups? I believe there can be, but the people of faith will first need to grasp the way the people of science think.

Largely this means using terms in the same way. As an illustration, let's take the term "creation science." Many scientists have trouble with such a term because the definition of [physical] science is "the observation, identification, description, experimental investigation and theoretical explanation of natural phenomena." The definition specifies that the scope of science is natural phenomena. Most scientists see an all-at-once creation as a supernatural event, one which is outside the scope of science. It is not outside the realm of possibility. We just cannot use natural methods to investigate it (at least at this point in time). Not all Christians realize this, and so there is more defensiveness than dialogue on the Christian side, and a lack of respect on the science side for Christians who do not check the definition.

This carries into debates over what can be taught in public schools. One reason there is objection to teaching creation in science classes in public schools is that creation is not seen as science. Creation might well be taught in public schools, but it would more properly come under the heading of a *worldview*. Teaching creation as a worldview would be acceptable to scientists.

My friend, Ralph Seelke, who heads up the Biology Department at the University of Wisconsin-Superior, makes an important observation: not all truth is scientific. By limiting itself to natural phenomena, science has not apprehended all the truth that there is. Science cannot explain, for example, the origin of life on earth. It has theories, but no solid proof of them. The origin of life remains a mystery and a miracle to scientists. Nor should the Church think it has the only truth. Because it believed mankind to be God's highest creation (which may be true), it once held that the earth was the center of our solar system (which was not true). If both scientists and people of faith are willing to expand their search for knowledge into a search for truth, a most excellent dialogue is possible.

And hopefully, in time, we will have a better picture of reality.

CIVILITY COVENANT (OR HOW TO BEHAVE AROUND ELECTION TIME)

In the spring preceding Barak Obama's election as President of the United States, a diverse group of us (more than 100 religious leaders) signed our names, committing us to a "Civility Covenant." We joined together recognizing that too often we have reflected the political divisions of our culture rather than the unity we have in the body of Christ. We came together to urge those who claim the name of Christ to "put away from you all bitterness and wrath and anger and wrangling and slander, together with all malice, and be kind to one another, tender-hearted, forgiving one another, as God in Christ has forgiven you" (Ephesians 4:31-32).

We made seven biblically based commitments which we hope will establish civility in American politics. Candidates need to know that we as voters do not just care about who wins, but how they win. The Civility Covenant states:

1. We commit that our dialogue with each other will reflect the spirit of the scriptures, where our posture toward each other is to be "quick to listen, slow to speak, and slow to become angry" (James 1:19).

2. We believe that each of us, and our fellow human beings, are created in the image of God. The respect we owe to God should be reflected in the honor and respect we show to each other in our common humanity, particularly in how we speak to each other. "With the tongue we bless the Lord and [God], and with it we curse those who are made in the likeness of God ... this ought not to be so" (James 3:9-10).

3. We pledge that when we disagree, we will do so respectfully, without falsely impugning the other's motives, attacking the other's character, or questioning the other's faith, and recognizing in humility that in our limited, human opinions, "we see but a poor reflection as in a mirror" (1 Corinthians 13:12). We will therefore "be completely humble and gentle; be patient, bearing with one another in love" (Ephesians 4:2).

4. We will ever be mindful of the language we use in expressing our disagreements, being neither arrogant nor boastful in our beliefs: "Before destruction one's heart is haughty, but humility goes before honor" (Proverbs 18:12).

5. We recognize that we cannot function together as citizens of the same community, whether local or national, unless we are mindful of how we treat each other in pursuit of the common good, in the common life we share together. Each of us must therefore "put off falsehood and speak truthfully to his neighbor, for we are all members of one body" (Ephesians 4:25).

6. We commit to pray for our political leaders — those with whom we may agree, as well as those with whom we may disagree. "I urge that supplications, prayers, intercessions, and thanksgivings be made— for kings and all who are in high positions" (1 Timothy 2:1-2).

7. We believe that it is more difficult to hate others, even our adversaries and our enemies, when we are praying for them. We commit to pray for each other, those with whom we agree and those with whom we may disagree, so that together we may strive to be faithful witnesses to our Lord, who prayed "that they may be one" (John 17:22).

We need to push back against the fear-mongering and name-calling and lead with our values, especially the value of civility.

CLOTHES MAKE THE MAN

Mark Twain (1835-1910) said that "clothes make the man," and followed up with "naked people have little or no influence on society." While his second statement is generally true, there are two naked people who did have a huge influence on society: Adam and Eve.

A Lutheran colleague and I were recently discussing the fall of mankind in the Garden of Eden. No, we don't always discuss biblical or spiritual things. Sometimes we talk about motorcycles or guitars or our families. But on this particular day we got into a great discussion about sin. In case you are wondering, we are both against it. The discussion ran along the lines of what sin does to people—how it leaves them exposed, naked and uncomfortable.

My friend thinks that Adam and Eve were not bothered by nakedness before they sinned because they were wearing the "clothes of righteousness" given to them by God when He created them. But after they sinned, they lost or forfeited those clothes and saw themselves and their birthday suits in a different light.

Their reaction was one of shame. And then they tried to make some new clothes for themselves. But fig leaves are not the Armani of the fashion world, and certainly are not comparable to the clothes of righteousness.

How wonderful that we don't have to stay in our sin, in our exposed and uncomfortable state. Honest confession coupled with trust in God brings a set of new clothes. Isaiah wrote, "I delight greatly in the LORD; my soul rejoices in my God. For He has clothed me with garments of salvation and arrayed me in a robe of righteousness."

Clothes may make a man (or woman) in an ordinary sense. But righteous clothes make a person in the best sense.

COLOR TAG

Over 100 elementary school boys and girls tensed at the edge of the upper field on a hot July day at Covenant Park Bible Camp in Mahtowa, Minnesota. I leaned forward with them and waited for the signal. "Blue!" yelled the athletic director. Like a shot, everyone wearing something blue dashed across the sunburned patch of ground to the other side screaming and squealing with delight. We weaved and dodged while counselors tried to tag us and make us "freeze."

It is called color tag, and if you are wearing the color that is called out, you have to run. I made it back and forth a couple more times with my young friends. And then the director called, "Gray!" I stood still. A small person looked up at me and said, "Run!" I checked my clothes. No gray. "Run!" said the small person again. I stood my ground. "You have to go!" the small person urged. "But I'm not wearing gray," I countered. "Uh huh...it's in your hair!" (Ouch!) I ran. I got caught too. There are moments in which you realize you've crossed a threshold. That was one such moment.

So I'm "old," at least in the eyes of some. In my mind I'm not much over thirty (while retaining the wisdom of my more than fifty years). But I am aging, and I am beginning to reflect on what I've accomplished so far.

Some guys have made a million dollars or started a company. Some of my peers have moved from small to medium to large churches or even into administrative positions in our denomination. I've never really sought that, but it makes me think.

Three things I know have changed with the march of time; four that make me happy. I know God better. I know His Word better. I'm more comfortable in my own skin. And I love people better than I used to. I am far from perfect. I know my faults well. But I am still running for my Lord. And gray is a good color to be wearing.

A COMPUTER RENAISSANCE

Until I recorded a music album, I don't think I properly appreciated geeks. There are some who work at a local store called Computer Renaissance. I've always been glad there were some geeks around, but necessity was never a mother to my invention like she was when I began recording. I purchased an eight-track digital recorder and set down some original songs based on Scripture and ministry experience. Some friends, who are good musicians, contributed to the project and it turned out pretty well. Recording is a blast and it's relatively easy. Making a CD, on the other hand...

If I had had an extra hundred dollars, I could have upgraded and bought a recorder with a CD burner. But I was living in the present at the time, not able to see into the future. It's like Yogi Berra said, "The future isn't what it used to be." So I didn't plan ahead.

It doesn't sound too hard to take an album on a recorder and send it to a computer, then burn a CD. But I found out that the recorder exports in WAVE format and CDs need to be in .mp3 format or there are too many megabytes for the CD to swallow. So you have to convert, which requires downloading a conversion program from cyberspace. And where is that really?

But I did it. By accident. And then, also by accident and sheer persistence, I lined the songs up the way I wanted and burned them onto a CD.

The next time I did it I wanted to do it on purpose, so I took notes. It takes thirty-seven steps. At least for me it does. Like I said, I don't think I properly appreciated geeks before this. I would never have known what it takes except that I had to do it. I had to become the geek. I could have had someone do the hard part for me, but I figured I needed to learn.

When God was figuring out how to provide salvation for the world, He didn't contract out the hard part—paying for the mistakes of the world. In the person of Jesus, He Himself became a human being and went through all the temptations we face, yet without giving in to them. He then offered His perfect life in payment for our less-than-perfect lives. You might say He offered to convert sinful WAVE people to forgiven .mp3 people. Jesus wrestled with doing this in the Garden of Gethsemane, asking if the suffering might pass from Himself to someone else. In contrast to how it is on the C\: drive, the conversion pain was very real. But in the end He took the suffering and died on the cross. His purpose in becoming a human being was to get to the cross.

I have no idea how many steps were in God's plan, but Jesus stayed true at every step and true to the entire plan. Those who trust in Jesus may enjoy the freedom of sins "deleted" from their lives and from God's memory as well. Jesus' resurrection on Easter clinched it. Death, the "fatal error," is the natural consequence of sin. And death claimed Jesus. But His resurrection was the "undo" of death. Or compare it to clicking on "restore" from the trash bin. While sins are not "restored," lives can be. This is God's domain, and

He never messes up, never "crashes," never gets a tension headache wondering where someone's information went.

Geeks are helpful. Extremely helpful. But God is essential. Computers route information through unseen places and make some things in life better and more enjoyable. But God routes salvation through Jesus and makes eternal life possible.

I don't know much about how computers work. Their binary minds are a mystery to me. God's mind is even more of a mystery. But I know from reading the Bible that He thinks about all of us. Because of His great love for us, He hopes that we will allow Him to do the "conversions" that we need. It is a renaissance that will allow us to really live.

CONCENTRATION

Out in the country, along desolate stretches of road with fields on both sides, you occasionally come to an intersection marked with white dust. Investigation will reveal that you are looking at ordinary baking flour. But why you would find flour there is hard to imagine... unless you also hear the drone of an airplane.

A friend, who is a pilot, got married. His best man was also a pilot, and during the best man's toast at the wedding reception, there was recollection of the two of them flying over intersections in the middle of nowhere, trying to land a bag of flour dead center on the meeting of the roads.

They also slipped balloons out the cockpit window and tried to come back around and chop them up with the propeller, which is tricky in a high wing craft because you are likely to lose sight of the balloon in the turn.

There are a number of physical laws to understand in order to be successful at flour dropping and balloon popping. The laws have to do with gravity, lift, air speed, wind vectors and the acceleration of falling objects. But even if a person understands these laws, he or she still needs the skill of concentration. Without concentration, no amount of aeronautical expertise will be of much benefit in plane games.

The Christian life requires concentration too. It requires an intense focus on the person of Jesus Christ. In our day of tolerance for almost anything, and of affirmation for so many different worldviews, concentrating on just one Savior may seem narrow, exclusive, arrogant or unwise.

I recall a radio spot in which a pilot was talking with the airport tower about where to land. Being a rugged individualist and the captain of his own destiny, he suggested a variety of open spaces. The tower, however, reminded him that he was flying a jumbo jet and that there was just one safe place to land—the airport, which had a runway long enough.

Jesus made a bold claim about Himself in John 14:6. He said, "I am the way, the truth and the life. No one comes to the Father except through Me." With allowances for those who have never heard the name of Jesus, and the Bible knows of such cases, it is a narrow choice of runways.

However, Paul said the same thing to his friend Timothy when he mentioned that "there is one God and one mediator between God and men, the man, Jesus Christ" (1 Timothy 2:5). Paul went on to say why Jesus is the only one: He "gave His life as a ransom for all men."

No one else in history has been a ransom for all men, paying for the sins of others with His own death. That is worth thinking about. And most religions admit that people cannot save themselves from sin and selfishness. So either sin has to be counted as nothing (everyone is excused, which is hard to fathom in the wake of great evil), or a ransom is needed.

But must a ransom be narrowed to just one person? Christian author and speaker C.S. Lewis was asked the question. He answered that if he were the devil, he thought he would do his best to convince people that there are many ways of salvation, so that most people would miss it. But if there is only one way of salvation, and a person finds it, he or she can be sure of it. Having only one way does actually make sense. It takes faith to see Jesus as the Savior of the world, although no more faith than many other things take, including atheism.

So many things in the world clamor for our attention. There is a lot of noise and busyness. Will we be able to concentrate on what is important? Concentrate on the proper target for faith? And on the safe runway? On the genuine way among many ways? On the ransom paid for us? On the Savior? God promises that everyone who earnestly looks for the Savior will find Him in Jesus.

CURT AND MELANIE

On December 9, 1988, three weeks before his wedding, Curt Vittitow's car was struck in the rear quarter panel half a block from his home in the Chicago area. The car spun around twice and smashed head-on into a tree in the median of the boulevard, buckling the vehicle. Curt's head snapped back and the fourth, fifth and sixth cervical vertebrae were broken. When Curt's father arrived at the scene of the accident just moments later, Curt was lying on the seat, his head hanging out the passenger door, his right knee wedged under the dash. He told his father, "I can't feel my legs."

The accident left Curt a quadriplegic. It changed Curt's whole life, except for two things. One was the love of a good woman. In rehab Curt and Melanie watched other relationships fall apart. Theirs didn't. Melanie took stock of their situation: Curt's body didn't do everything that it had done before, but he was still the man with whom she had fallen in love. Same heart, same spirit. And she wanted him as much as he wanted her. After six months of rehabilitation, on June 17, 1989, Curt and Melanie took their marriage vows.

The other thing that didn't change was Curt's sense of humor. With minimal use of his shoulders, scratching an itch on his head was a trick. He would jerk a shoulder and fling an arm up, sometimes whacking it on the headboard of the bed. "Wow!" he would say, "I'll bet that hurt!" Of course he couldn't feel a thing. Racing around the house in his motorized wheelchair, he would crash into a wall and get stuck there. "Mel," he would call, "could you come and straighten out my foot?" New caregivers would often be asked to scratch an itch on his knee, until Melanie would pop into the room and ask what they were doing. When they explained, Melanie would remind them that Curt was a quadriplegic. Then it would dawn on them that they had been the object of his joke. And he would grin mischievously.

On their thirteenth anniversary, Melanie came home and opened the front door. She smelled the sweet fragrance of roses. Thirteen dozen roses. One dozen for each of their years together, each bunch with a card conveying Curt's affection and appreciation. Melanie was overwhelmed.

Curt passed away at the age of forty-two of respiratory failure. It was the conclusion to a long series of health struggles. He died in Melanie's arms and went into the waiting arms of Jesus. He did not live a long life, but he lived a full one. There wasn't much that he wouldn't try, including teaching Melanie to rollerblade. He pulled her behind his wheelchair until she got the hang of it.

What comes across from Melanie is a deep sense of satisfaction and of gratitude when she looks back over their marriage. Faith, family and tenacity were the keys. Many times prayer made the difference between life and death for Curt. Many times family members rushed to help in a crisis. Many times Melanie pushed an ER technician out of the way to do something for Curt that only she knew how to do.

It wasn't an easy life, but it was a life worth all the trouble. In a time when so many couples are deciding they cannot make a go of it, Curt and Melanie decided they could not give up. What they had has a name: true love. Of this kind of love the Apostle Paul had a comment: "[It] never fails" (1 Corinthians 13:8).

DEER HUNTING PHILOSOPHY

The women of my church hosted a Sportsmen's chili dinner for the men. After three kinds of chili, toppings, salad, cornbread and too many desserts to really be good for us, we pulled our chairs into a circle and shared some of our outdoor adventures. Some terrific stories were told.

There was the one about the bear that interrupted a deer hunter and refused to quit making scary noises even after it was dead. And the one about the bear that interrupted a fishing trip and ended up in the cooler with the fillets. Lots of deer hunting yarns were spun too. And my friend, Harold, casually remarked during the course of the evening that he has taken over fifty deer. That may be about average for around here, but it was a wonderment to me.

I came into hunting late, not having done it while growing up. My father did not hunt, and so I picked it up from friends and from my stepfather-in-law, who became my hunting partner. "Vegetarian," when translated in some of the Native American dialects means "man who has not yet shot a deer," and that is what I was for quite some time.

It wasn't for lack of trying. For seven seasons I worked at it. In my first season I borrowed a Winchester

94 from my buddy Don, and sneaked around the woods near Barr's Lake in northern Minnesota. The next year I borrowed another 94 with a scope. I learned how to use a rifle with a scope after blackening my right eye. The year after that I bought my own 94 with a Williams peep sight and didn't hurt myself. The fourth year I moved to a Remington bolt-action 260 with a synthetic stock and got a shot off in the forest around Saginaw. The doe I was aiming at looked me over and judged I wouldn't be able to hit her if she jumped. I hate it when deer just know. The next year was the same, only without a shot. Then I needed a riding lawn mower, so I sold my rifle to my friend, Rob, and went to an inexpensive 1922 Australian Enfield in .303 British caliber. That year I had a doe in my sights at thirty yards and fired the shot that couldn't miss. My friend Tedd helped me track the doe until we concluded that, in my excitement, I had jerked and fired high. There was a tuft of hair though . . . with a deer tick on it. "Wow!" said Tedd, "You shot a tick off the back of a deer!" I felt better after that. The seventh year, there were no shots fired. But a buck came up the trail after legal shooting hours and laughed at me. All those years I kept getting closer. In the eighth year I bought a Browning lever-action .243 and was resolved that it would happen, which it did. My wife figures it was one of the most expensive deer ever taken.

While I was waiting on that deer, I gained some things that are priceless, like time spent with my stepfather-in-law and some good friends in very beautiful surroundings. Patience paid off. Perseverance had its reward.

How true that is for spiritual things. Those who trust in Jesus are not automatically good at living the Christian life. It is especially challenging for those who start later in life. We would like to do it well, have the character and values of Jesus the first season. We would like to move forward constantly, in a straight line, but for most of us it is more like riding one of those amusement park rides that goes in a corkscrew, only in the Christian life, we go backwards too. But by working at the basics—studying God's Word, talking with Him and listening to Him, spending time with other Christians, and sharing with others what we are learning—we come to maturity. Patience pays off. Perseverance has its reward.

In my young adulthood I chose a life verse from the Bible, something to guide me as I navigate the world. It is my philosophy for living the Christian life. It comes from Luke 9:62 and says, "No one who puts his hand to the plow and looks back is fit for service in the kingdom of God." In other words, don't give up. God always gives us what we need to make it through. Keep at it, even in the times of doubt.

It's a good philosophy for hunting deer too.

DESPAIR AND HOPE

For over a year we prayed for the grandson of one of our church couples. And we were not alone. Thousands of people all over the country petitioned God on his behalf. Gabe got a rare kind of cancer at age six. Medical teams at several hospitals made heroic efforts. His mother donated stem cells. "Soldiers" to fight the cancer she called them. And the cancer went into remission (see the essay entitled "Bull Moose"). But in the end, a rejection of those cells, called graft versus host disease, took Gabe's life.

Radio preacher Chuck Swindoll says there are three accelerants of despair: suddenness, severity and settlement. We are pushed into a negative frame of mind when something happens suddenly, unexpectedly. And we are dragged down when the thing that happens is severe and painful. And we are pulled into despair when the event is settled or set in a way that cannot be changed. Gabe's death was all of that: sudden, severe and settled.

Of course it doesn't seem fair, and we wonder if God is fair. Christians believe that God is powerful enough to heal, but that did not happen. And like Job in the Old Testament, we don't always get answers to the questions searing our sensibilities like a hot iron.

Some of us get angry with God for not intervening, and for not answering our questions about why He didn't intervene. I asked God some pointed questions about Gabe. I did not get the answers I sought. Only this from God: "Gabe is safe in My hands."

During our summer vacation in Michigan, we visited some friends who adopted a little boy named Luke. Luke was younger than Gabe, only four years old. Luke's biological mother was addicted to meth. So Luke was born addicted too. He was also born with a large birthmark, almost a "horn" on his forehead, which is slowly receding. He was not expected to walk. He was not expected to see. Doctors removed blood from behind Luke's eyes, so that he might have the chance to apprehend light and shadow, nothing more. But Luke has sight. And he is walking. His parents prayed. Other people prayed, and Luke is getting well.

Luke's mother decided to look up his "birthday verse." He was born on July 22, so his mother looked up the Gospel of Luke, chapter 7, verse 22. In that verse, Jesus tells the disciples of John the Baptist what is happening in Jesus' ministry so that John can know if Jesus is the Messiah, the One promised by God to be the Savior of the world. Jesus says, "Go your way, and tell John what things you have seen and heard; how the blind see, the lame walk . . ." It fit Luke perfectly.

I am happy for Luke and his parents. They have witnessed a miracle. And I grieve with Gabe's parents and grandparents. For them the miracle was so close ... Gabe's death pulls me toward despair. Luke's healing propels me toward hope. I don't know how God runs the universe. I just know that trusting Him is much better than not trusting Him. Even people who are healed will die sometime. What happens after a person is done living, however long or short the lifespan, matters most.

I don't know how God figures out a person's lifespan. I just know that I can see Luke now, and though my heart aches for Gabe, I will see him later, in eternity. Gabe is more healed now than he ever would have been on earth. Young as he was, he knew that's how it would be and said so.

My wife and I have talked a lot about the ways of God in these matters. She keeps a journal. In it are her conversations with God. She gave me permission to share what she wrote about death and healing, despair and hope. She writes to God, "The point for me is not whether or not You heal people and how often, and how serious the affliction, and the age of the sick person, and how many people witness the healing [if it happens]. The point is that death is not—will never be—the final word. The final Word [Jesus Christ, Who rose from the dead] is our hope. And that is the Gospel."

That *is* the Gospel.

DOES THE DEAD PERSON QUALIFY?

When my father passed away in October of 2010, we learned it was his wish to donate his body to science. He lived in Fort Smith, Arkansas, and people there who become anatomical donations go to the Medical Center at the University of Arkansas at Little Rock. The local funeral director, who was helping us with arrangements, told us that there were some qualifications. My brother made the necessary calls and this is what he found out about the qualifications.

To become an anatomical donation you must meet three criteria: you must be refrigerated, you must not be obese and you must not have any infectious, communicable diseases at the time of death. My father met all the criteria and so was qualified. He made a scientific contribution after he passed from this world.

Every one of us is going to die someday. Most of us hope it isn't today, or soon, but the day will come. Not everyone wishes to donate his or her body to science and so doesn't have to worry about the qualifications which pertain to medical centers. But what about the qualifications for being accepted into heaven? What does God ask of persons entering into eternity?

Atheists, who do not believe that God exists, assume that this life is all there is. In their view no one qualifies for heaven because heaven does not exist, just as God does not exist. Agnostics say that God and heaven might exist, but maybe not, and there is no sure way to know. They remain skeptical that there is any spiritual geography, and figure that heaven is a manmade construct rather than a real place. On the other side of the divide, some people think that everyone is qualified for heaven. These folks, called Universalists, believe that people are automatically qualified by being part of the human race—that God in His goodness could not consign anyone to hell, so everyone goes to heaven. This is an attractive idea, but overlooks the injustice of excusing those who have lived resolutely evil lives. But most people, even in religions other than Christianity, think going to heaven is a matter of being good. For them "good" is defined in a relative way, in comparison to others who are obviously "worse," and the measuring stick is usually their own "good" selves.

None of these, however, is the idea that God Himself gives us in His account of The Way Things Are, as recorded in the Bible. In the Bible we find just one qualification for going to heaven: that a person trusts in Jesus and reverences Him as Lord. In the Gospel of John these words of Jesus are set down for us: "I tell you the truth, whoever hears My word and believes Him Who sent Me has eternal life and will not be condemned; he has crossed over from death to life" (John 5:24).

This trust in Jesus usually comes with the awareness of a need to trust Him because of sins committed that cannot be undone or excused by the person himself or herself. The "gospel" or good news is that Jesus is willing to "change clothes" with us. He puts on our "guilty clothes," allowing us to put on His "innocent clothes" when we express our trust in Him. His death on the cross was His way of paying for our sins in the "guilty clothes." His resurrection shows that death could not make a permanent claim on Him, and the good news says that death cannot make a permanent claim on anyone else trusting in Him.

Some people think that simple trust is too simple, and so reject the one qualifier which God gives us. But it makes perfect sense. God keeps it simple because He wants everyone to qualify for heaven. Every dead person can go. The catch is that we have to trust in Jesus while we are still alive.

EASTER FAITH IN GOOD FRIDAY PEOPLE

I conducted a funeral for a friend named Matt. He was only twenty-eight—a closer friend to my twenty-four year old son, but my friend too. He lived at my son's group home on the east side of Duluth, Minnesota.

Matt was born with a Dandy Walker cyst at the base of his brain. He also had cerebral palsy. His walking and thinking were affected. And because of needing a breathing tube on several occasions, his speech was raspy. He had these disabilities, but they in no way impacted his ability to receive God's love or his ability to place his trust in Christ for the forgiveness of his sins.

Matt loved music, B.J. Thomas in particular. He was a car nut. And he loved practical jokes. Ordinary people made him light up, and if he had been waiting to see you, the entire house knew of your arrival, as if you were royalty. Who doesn't like being treated like royalty once in a while?

Late in May and late at night, Matt had a seizure. It was a big one. He had had them before, but this one was different. He slipped into a coma and didn't come out. His heart and lungs were too weak to recover. He died in the hospital, surrounded by family and some friends, as dawn was breaking over the city. The nurses began to use heroic measures to revive him. His mother and father courageously said, "Let him go."

At his funeral we played his favorite Christian music. One of his group home staff members made a slide show of his life that ran while the music played. Everyone loved the picture showing his big smile, mischief playing at the corners of his mouth and a twinkle in his eyes. His uncle and I both spoke. But the best part of the service was when his peers got up to pay tribute.

His peers have disabilities like Matt—Cerebral Palsy, Down's syndrome, blindness. Some had to walk carefully to the platform and up the steps. None was a bit hesitant though. To a person they spoke of faith—an Easter resurrection faith, from their imperfect Good Friday bodies, to borrow a phrase from C. John Weborg, a seminary professor of mine. They were eloquent. I'm not saying they seemed eloquent. I'm telling you they were eloquent, as eloquent as able-bodied persons. It was as if, for a few minutes, they had no developmental challenges.

The ability of these peers to speak about God and about their faith and about Matt's faith was better than any well-crafted apologetic I have heard. What they said was simple and it was direct, the way Jesus was simple and direct. Their words revealed something that brilliant minds don't always grasp: the joy of hearts and wills solidly given over to God. The strength of their testimony was undeniable. The truth of their witness was irrefutable.

The Apostle Paul wrote to his friends in the city of Corinth, Greece, "... God chose the foolish things of the world to shame the wise" (1 Corinthians 1:27). Much of what developmentally challenged people do probably seems like foolishness to more able-bodied folks. The "damage" they carry around with them makes able-bodied folks pay less attention to them or give condescending attention to them. But those peers of Matt's, who know and live for God, are so wise.

Easter faith sometimes comes inside wounded, scarred and damaged Good Friday people. And the world is richer for it.

FIRST FISH

Her name is Emily and she was six years old. Our church family was spending the weekend on retreat at Covenant Park Bible Camp in Mahtowa, Minnesota, located on Park Lake. There was a compost pile and so there were worms. There was a fishing pole and so ...

I put the worm on the hook for her amid lots of comments about the worm. I showed her how to push the line release with her thumb and let it up so the hook, worm and bobber landed in the water. We were standing on a dock and a whole school of sunfish was watching the proceedings with great anticipation. These particular sunfish were quite adept at stealing the bait.

The rest happened pretty fast! There was a splash, and instantaneously there was a sunfish bigger than all the rest, swimming in all directions at once and wondering why the bait was refusing to be swallowed. Emily was holding on for dear life, wild shrieks coming out of her mouth and all her concentration centered on that fish. After a few fiercely intense moments, calm prevailed. The fish was landed, unhooked and ceremoniously placed in a bucket of lake water, much awe accompanying the ministrations.

Her father, who had been packing the motor coach, was the first outside the immediate gathering to hear of her good fortune. "How did you do it?" he inquired. "I really don't know," she replied. She was telling the truth.

Emily returned to the Arena of Excitement a few minutes later and landed another equally wonderful sunfish. "That's good!" I said. "Brilliant!" she corrected me. For many days after the BIG DAY, she pressed her dad to take her fishing. Can you blame her?

Some folks meet God the way Emily met her fish: in an exhilarating rush of furious excitement. They don't always know how it happened. But there is enough evidence "in the bucket" to know it is real. They know they want to keep meeting with God too, over and over. And He is always happy to oblige.

GOOD FRIDAY AT THE ABORTION CLINIC

This devotion was delivered at the Building for Women in Downtown Duluth, Minnesota on Good Friday, 2011, where abortions are performed, and where a prayer vigil for the unborn is held each year.

After Jesus was arrested in the Garden of Gethsemane, he stood trial twice. He was tried the first time before Jewish authorities, who charged Him with blasphemy (lying about being God). It was incomprehensible to them that He might be God and a human being at the same time, although this was true.

He was tried a second time before Roman authorities, because under imperial law the Jews as a conquered people could not exercise the death penalty, and they needed the Romans to carry out the sentence they wanted. Pilate, the Roman governor, realized during the interrogation that there was no basis for a charge deserving death, and tried to release Jesus. But the crowds were agitated, and threatening to riot. They cleverly shifted their charge to that of treason (that Jesus, the "King" of the Jews, was somehow a threat to Caesar, which was not true). Under pressure, Pilate folded and Jesus was condemned to death by crucifixion. He was crucified on the day we call Good Friday. But two different times during the Roman trial Pilate said to the crowd, "I find no basis for a charge against Him" (John 18:38 and John 19:6).

When a baby is conceived there is often great joy in a home. But sometimes there is not. There is great agitation instead. Sometimes there are unhappy discussions and yelling and anger and sorrow and hard questions.

Man: "How did this happen?"

Woman: "Well, a few weeks ago you were feeling amorous..."

Man: "I know **how** it happened! What I mean is **why** did it happen? Didn't you use protection?"

Woman: "Didn't you?"

And we wonder, along with Mother Teresa, what is so scary about an infant that we would have to protect ourselves from such a tiny person?

Emotions escalate and events move toward a trial. Not a formal one, but a trial just the same. The man, though partly responsible, does not go on trial. And the woman, though partly responsible (except in cases of rape or incest) does not go on trial either. But the woman is usually put on the witness stand several times. No, it is the child, growing inside the woman, who is put on trial.

An impartial observer would be right to say about the child, "I find no basis for a charge ..." And yet, under pressure from the man, from family members, from professional counselors, from friends, maybe from the woman too, efforts to set the child free are often abandoned, and the child is handed over to "executioners." And Good Friday, the day on which an innocent person was put to death, comes again and again to our world. In Duluth it happens, on average, fifteen times each week.

And yet there is hope. Addressing the universal need in His own day, and anticipating the need in ours, Jesus said from the cross, "Father, forgive them, for they do not know what they are doing" (Luke 23:34). These words changed the world. These words are still changing the world every time someone seeks forgiveness for abortion, or anything else for that matter. Even better is the hope we have because of Jesus' resurrection. His resurrection from the dead gives us the assurance that, though innocent lives are lost in our time, they are not lost forever. In the time He chooses, innocent souls will live again. Meanwhile, we struggle on bravely, seeking to end injustice against those who have no voice but ours.

GREEN LIGHT, RED LIGHT

One Thanksgiving holiday I reconfigured the Lionel train layout in my basement. For about nine years I had worked with two intersecting loops, trying to puzzle out how to run two trains simultaneously, which the old manual from the 1960's said I could do. Last year I got it, using some insulating connectors and a second transformer. But the layout was small, shoehorned into the space between the furnace and a wall, so even if I switched like mad, the trains were prone to crash.

The new layout was better: Two completely separate loops, one inside the other, each on its own transformer. It was still in the same small space, so I had to be careful to allow enough room to let the trains pass each other. The inside loop also got a side spur—a railroad yard parking space.

As I was changing things around I accidentally broke the switch arrow that shows which way the turnout track will send a train on the inner loop. They don't make the arrows anymore, so I was sorry for the loss. But there is a wonderful store in the Lincoln Park area—Carr's Hobby Shop which is crammed from floor to ceiling with planes, trains, cars, ships, scenery, paint, tiny people, tanks, the odd Whizzer bike, balsa wood, almost anything you can think of. And Jack, the owner, had a couple of switch arrows. He also had a Lionel ZW transformer, which made my eyes light up. Some unused birthday money was soon spent, and I commenced replacing the arrows and hooking up the new transformer.

The ZW runs both trains (it would run four if I had two more), blows the whistles, allows trains to change directions ... it's an amazing thing! It also has two lights on it, one green and one red. And only the green one was working. I fiddled and fussed, re-wired and changed the bulbs around, tried different connector posts, all to no avail. Finally I called Jack. "The red light won't come on," I complained. "I hope not!" Jack replied. "It only comes on when there's an electrical short somewhere. It's a warning light." "Oh," I said. (I have a facility for intelligent language when I am embarrassed.) Nothing was wrong; all was as it should be. I had fretted needlessly.

Do you ever do that? Get bent out of shape only to find that no disaster has occurred, that the impending doom is not pending at all? And along the way, in your alarm, sometimes blow up at the people around you, damaging relationships and looking foolish?

Jesus gave good counsel about life, about things that we think have happened or might happen which we believe will make tomorrow miserable. He said, "Do not worry about tomorrow, for tomorrow will worry about itself. Each day has enough trouble of its own" (Matthew 6:34). It came as a surprise when someone told me that worry is a form of not trusting God, but it's true.

Holidays, like Thanksgiving, are stressful for many people. Regular days are too. But God can transform a troubled mind into a trusting mind. He can do it even for the person who is really good at worrying! If the red light is not on, relax and enjoy the people around you. Mark Twain once said, "I've spent a lot of time worrying about things that never happened to me." I have too. But I'm asking God to change that.

Life is better when lived in the glow of a green light.

HINTS LYING AROUND

Sometimes the question washes over me like a wave: Could something as unusual as resurrection from the dead be real? Luke 1:37 anchors me in the truth that yes, resurrection from the dead is real. It says, "Nothing is impossible with God." But how does it happen? What makes it reasonable to believe?

God in His goodness has left hints lying around in the physical world. I think it was important to Him that we "get it," that we be able to apprehend what is easy for Him to understand and accomplish, but is a mystery to us.

A seed is "buried" in the ground. "Dead" over a period of time, it is raised to life, pushes out of the ground and grows into a plant, with a new kind of body, just as the Scriptures say we will have someday if we have died "in Christ."

A bird lays an egg. To all appearances it is "dead." But a baby bird is raised to life, pecks its way out of the shell and strengthens itself to eventually fly, just as the Scriptures say we will do in some fashion when we are caught up to heaven with Jesus. A caterpillar finds a leaf, spins a "tomb," and a couple seasons later is raised to new life as a new creature with wonderful new abilities, just as the Scriptures say we will have when Christ raises us to new life.

Three different life forms in the natural world—plants, birds and insects—all confirm the words of Scripture to people whom God loves and wishes to redeem.

On Google Images I found pictures of a coconut sprouting, baby birds hatching in their nest and a Cecropia moth in various stages of development—a plant, a bird, an insect. I printed them and took them to Bible study at the North Place group home where my son, Ryan, lives. The guys had a great time identifying the pictures. But more importantly, we all were helped in faith by these hints, just lying around, of new life springing from "death," of resurrection—the unusual, mysterious event we look forward to—because nothing is impossible with God.

HOW DID THEY *DO* THAT?

When I get a chance, I visit historical sites and learn about life in a different time. I am curious by nature, and touring a mansion from yesteryear, like the Congdon family's Glensheen, or the lower level of the Duluth Depot with its steam locomotives, snowplow, shops and model railroad display fill me with deep pleasure. I read the cards that tell about the things I am seeing and I soak in as much as I can. I especially like old tools. One of my favorite books is by Eric Sloan, who drew and described tools used by the pioneers and settlers of our country. At garage sales I gravitate to old tools, and if I cannot identify one, I must buy it. If I cannot figure it out, I find an old timer who knows what it is and probably used it. Good stories always come with the explanations.

Tools come in all sizes, and I was looking at quite a variety recently at Tom's Logging Camp between Duluth and Two Harbors, Minnesota. One of the larger tools, in a picture, was a sled piled to an almost unbelievable height with logs from a white pine forest. The actual sled, minus its load, rested quietly in a barn. Two or possibly four horses would pull such a sled with up to five tons of weight. How did they *do* that? I had seen similar pictures but couldn't figure out how just a couple of horses could manage to move the load.

In another part of the camp I got my answer. Next to a different kind of sled, topped with a large wooden water tank, there was a card and a picture. The display told how loggers waited for the ground to freeze and the snow to fall and then constructed an ice road. They used a piece of iron twisted into a lopsided U shape to dig out a rut on each side of the road. Then horses pulled the water wagon down the road and a bung or plug was pulled to let water leak out of the bottom of the tank and into the ruts. The water froze and made two rails of ice for the log sled to slide on. Getting started was a bit of a trick, but once underway, the sled with five tons of logs went along quite nicely. It went too nicely on hills, which posed a hazard. So straw was spread on the ice to slow the sled down.

Each of us has some very difficult things to do or go through in life. As if trying to move an enormous load of logs, we wonder how we are going to manage. In Genesis 18:14 God asks the patriarch Abraham, "Is anything too hard for the LORD?" In Jeremiah 32:27 God says to the prophet Jeremiah, "I am the LORD, the God of all mankind. Is anything too hard for me?" It may not always be obvious to us, but God has a way of doing things that will ease our burden, smooth the way and get us where we need to go. Like an ice road for the loggers, God knows how to reduce the friction we experience and help us arrive safely at the right destination, even when our load is particularly heavy and when we are traveling too fast for our own good.

We cannot always choose the road we must take, or the load we must bear. But we can choose a Companion who knows how to do what we do not know how to do. Nothing is too hard for Him.

I DON'T WAVE ON THE BRIDGE

I am always sad when the motorcycle riding season draws to a close. Long and pleasant summers are hard to beat.

There is a kinship among riders, a kind of brotherhood and sisterhood, and an informal code of the road. Most bikers passing each other acknowledge each other with a wave. When someone unfamiliar with riding asks about this, I just say we all know each other. We do not of course, but it adds to the mystique of riding.

We wave in many different ways. Left arm extended down with an index finger pointing at the road, an open palm as if we were going to slap hands in passing, a high five. In the middle of clutching or if there is a vintage bike with a shifter knob, the "wave" might be just a nod of the head.

But there are times we excuse ourselves from waving. At night for example, when we are wearing black leather, no one can see more than headlights, so we don't wave. In the middle of turns when both hands, both feet and both eyes are busy with braking, clutching, shifting and looking, we don't wave. And when it is very windy we don't wave either.

Wind is not the friend of a biker. I have been hit by crosswinds on the John A. Blatnik Bridge between Duluth, Minnesota and Superior, Wisconsin. The bike slides a little, getting too close to the concrete barrier which separates me from the gray, choppy waters below. At times like these, when I am concentrating on staying upright, ten white knuckles grabbing the handlebars, I excuse myself from waving on the bridge.

It puzzles me that Christians, some of whom have been "riding" the Christian life for years, "wave" and let go of reality with one or even both hands, in a crosswind of deception. Maybe I shouldn't be so surprised. Our Enemy is skilled at making unsound and dangerous ideas (the Church calls them "heresies") seem good, even desirable. There is always just enough truth in them to fool people.

Mature Christians, however, check curious ideas against God's Word. They exercise the spiritual gift of discernment. And they choose to belong to a local fellowship which is less likely than an individual to be taken in. And fortunately, most heresies take one of just a couple forms:

1. That Jesus is not fully God (and the variation that mankind may attain Godhood).
2. That Jesus was not fully human.

If an exciting new teaching can be framed in one of these two heretical ways, you do not have to wave at it. The truth is that Jesus is fully God and He was fully human while on earth. And no one blows over while keeping a firm grip on that with both hands and a heart.

ICE AND WATER

Installing an elevated lift in our church building necessitated putting on an addition at the end of the Fellowship Hall. Offices displaced by the remodeling went into the new wing. And the library moved upstairs into the addition as well. Everyone liked the way it turned out.

The new section was created by digging a U-shaped trench below the frost line, then pouring a concrete footing in the trench, then building a block wall to just above ground level. After that a stud wall was built, and roof trusses were set on top of the wall. The roof was sheeted with 3/4" CDX (plywood), and on top of the sheeting went a special shield called Ice and Water. The metal roof was screwed down on top of that, and attractive stone block was laid on the outside of the stud wall. A poured floor with in-floor heating was added and the whole area was finished with sheetrock and carpet.

Everything about the project interested me, but it was the special roof shield that most captured my attention. Called Ice and Water, it prevents ice dams and water leaks. It is made of rubberized asphalt and not only adheres to the roof sheeting, but also seals around the screws used to attach the metal roof which goes on top of it. It is, in the words of the contractor, the "second line of defense" against the weather, after the metal roof.

In the spiritual world, Jesus is like the metal roof—the first line of defense against the storms of life. And Christians are like the Ice and Water shield, the second line of defense. They have the protection of the Savior, and also provide protection for each other through discernment, godly counsel, practical help, even intervention on occasion. Some "weather" comes the way of every church, from the world and from the Enemy, so Christians ought not to generate their own storms. Or leave each other exposed to damaging elements by spiritual "leaks" commonly known as gossip. Just as the Ice and Water shield needs to have integrity and cover all of a roof, Christians must have integrity and cover all of a local church. This requires taking appropriate responsibility for each other, overlooking some faults while not letting folks get away with bad behavior, showing a lot of love and constantly checking the "blueprint" (God's word) to see how best to do the covering and protecting. Getting it right is not easy, but the result—a strong, well-protected "building"—is well worth the effort.

Oh, the reason the Ice and Water shield captured my attention? It was because it is made by the Grace Construction Company.

IF ROOFING WERE AN OLYMPIC EVENT...

If roofing were an Olympic event, our church could compete.

Our head deacon was diagnosed with bilateral neck cancer. He suffered through grueling radiation treatments and chemotherapy, including a new experimental medicine. The cancer is gone, but the life-saving regimen almost killed him. He was very happy to be alive, but his body took a while to get happy. When he discovered that his roof, which he and his wife put on themselves, had sun and hail damage, he realized that he would not be putting on the new one.

Another man in church, with experience in building, jumped on the opportunity. He organized a work party. His wife organized lunch for the crew. Materials were ordered. While it was still dark, folks drove to the home, got on their mark, and got set. At seven o'clock the starting nail gun went off.

Shingle shovels scraped like mad. Bundles of old shingles were scooped up and tossed off the roof into a dumpster, with ground spotters calling out the degree of difficulty for each toss and scores for hitting the dumpster. "Ice and Water" fairly flew onto the eaves.

Tar paper rolled across the prepped and swept plywood. Drip edge was measured, fitted, cut and nailed. And then the real work began with the laying of the new shingles. Some people hauled, some set them in place, four people nailed as air compressors buzzed and puffed. It was an amazing team. In all, twenty-nine people contributed to the effort, with about fifteen on the roof at any given time.

There was a moment when it looked like we might forfeit our bid for a medal. A difference of opinion surfaced as to how best to go around the metal chimney. Some thought the entire flashing from the chimney should go under the shingles, with caulk around the stack making a water-tight seal. Others thought the bottom half of the chimney flashing should go on top of the shingles so water would have no chance to get under anything. This reasoning was equally strong. There was a pause, all eyes intensely fixed on the chimney. In that moment we understood why there are Covenanters *and* Baptists. The flashing-under faction acquiesced in true Christian humility, and the flashing-over faction proceeded to its work without gloating. (In the after-event debriefing it was concluded that God did not have a preference).

Finally, roof vents and ridge cap shingles were secured, with some artistry where a gable peak joined the southern slope. At five o'clock, exactly ten hours from the starting gun, the job was finished and the crowd in the stands (mainly the food servers and home-owners) leapt to their feet cheering wildly. The team was triumphant. Huge smiles beamed down from the roof. There were no sports network interviews. No actual medals. Still, everyone knew that greatness had been achieved. The Church had been the Church, in one of its best incarnations. We had worked together well, doing something that mattered. Our focus had been on others. We had set out to love, as we had been loved by God, and we had loved well.

We don't always love the way God loves. Sometimes we fail miserably. But sometimes we shine. And this time, although the place and the degree of sacrifice were quite different, there were nails, just like the time God loved us best of all at Calvary.

IGNORANCE OF
THE LAW IS NO EXCUSE

Two teenagers in our house completed the classroom part of their driver's training course and were eager to get out on the road. They practiced in the church parking lot all winter and did not hit the telephone pole in the center of it, which I counted as a good thing. They quizzed each other on signs, speed limits, safe driving practices, the folly of not wearing seat belts, and how seriously a person can be injured at a really low speed. And they showed interest in learning how to change a tire, jump-start a stalled vehicle, and add coolant to the radiator. They were diligent to point out that I should have checked over my right shoulder when backing up, and they noticed when, if there had been a pedestrian in the crosswalk, I would have run him over because I stopped two feet further ahead than I should have. I used to be asked, "Dad, do you know where you are going?" But after the teenagers got permits, an invisible sign appeared on the back of my head which read, "How's my driving? Let me know."

Those of us who have been driving for some time may have forgotten how much there is to know, and how much of it is confusing. We have picked up a lot of knowledge over time, and made some mistakes that heightened our awareness of what it takes to be a good driver. Each new situation has a learning curve.

When we lived in Chicago, and I began driving a delivery van for a company that distributed plastic laminate to cabinet shops, I wanted to do a good job for my employer, including saving time on routes. One day I lost time because I got a ticket for driving on Lake Shore Boulevard. I had missed the "No Commercial Vehicles" sign at the entrance. I found out that ignorance of the law is no excuse, and I had to appear in court. I imagine my offspring will learn a similar lesson at some point.

Ignorance of God's law is also no excuse for not-so-good behavior. God establishes laws, especially regarding love for others, so that we will not hurt each other or tarnish the image of God placed within all of us. The "rule of the road" given by Jesus is "Do unto others as you would have them do unto you" (Matthew 7:12). Jesus said this sums up the entire "Driver's Manual"—the Law and the Prophets.

Failure to consider others, to be kind, to go out of our way to help, to be our brother's keeper, to forgive, to love, to rein in our temper, to do good when it is within our power, to watch our language, to tell the truth, to be humble, to be content with what we have, to be accountable ... is serious stuff. It is like leaving the scene of a traffic accident without rendering aid. The Holy Spirit writes "tickets" on our conscience for such failures, and we have to appear in God's "court." Happily, the Judge is also our loving Father and there is much leniency and grace, even if we are repeat offenders.

Those of us with young adult children hope they become good drivers. We hope they are attentive and conscientious. We hope they are courteous and drive defensively. We hope even more that they do well on life's highway and follow the "rule of the road" given them by Jesus. We hope that they realize their tongues are every bit as powerful as a two ton iron thing on wheels and we hope that they avoid "accidents."

On the Minnesota roads we have a family rule: no talking or texting on a cell phone while driving! But we let family members pray, provided they keep their eyes open!

INDOCTRINATION AND EDUCATION

God has favored the human race with enormous freedom of choice. This freedom is both a privilege and a curse. With it we can do enormous good. But it is enough to destroy ourselves.

I am not in favor of less freedom for human beings as a way of preventing poor choices. And I am not in favor of *indoctrination* in the Church in the interest of preserving souls, indoctrination being the teaching of just one side of things to the exclusion of other sides. While that may seem wise, it does not serve people well when they encounter the world's ideas and have no adequate defense against them. What I do favor is *education*, the teaching of both sides of an issue, with consideration given to the age and maturity of those being taught, and with reasonable, biblical explanations for why Christian ideas are more sensible.

Josh McDowell wrote some excellent books explaining and defending the Christian Faith. When he came to our town, he told a group of ministers that young people are not much influenced by admonitions such as "because the Bible says so." A heavy-handed approach is not effective, except in the most square-cornered families and fellowships. The reason we follow what the Bible recommends, he said, is because the values taught in the Bible are based on the character of God. We are trying to be like Him; we are not just trying to adhere to printed rules. I have never known God to be intimidated by discussions with more than one side. He is not made small by other worldviews. I think He welcomes the chance to show why He "is God and apart from [Him] there is no Savior" (Isaiah 43:11). We need not be intimidated on God's behalf. Christians need not be afraid of questions and open conversation.

A "university" is an institution of higher learning in which there is a diversity of ideas. Lots of questions are asked. Lots of ideas are explored. It seems to me that the Church should be similar, a safe place, if you will, for everyone to ask questions, even hard questions. In the Church, if we do not know an answer, we should be honest enough to say so, and motivated enough to look into it.

People rarely ask purely academic questions. For example, when someone wants to know if you are always saved once you are saved, it is usually because someone else in the family made a commitment to Jesus, walked away and then died suddenly. The inquirer wants to know: What is the state of the person's soul now? That is not an easy question to answer; and it is certainly not hypothetical.

The difference between the Church and the university lies in their foundations. The university rests on the foundation of ideas in general, but the Church rests on the foundation of Jesus—His character, His values, His word.

The Church has long been "in the business" of Christian Education. Over the years, Christian Education has been called Sunday School or Church

School or Christian Formation or Discipleship or Lifelong Learning or something else. But all of the terms mean education. Sadly the Church has sometimes resorted to indoctrination and to the establishing of litmus tests to make sure people are thinking rightly. Right thinking is crucial, but right thinking through indoctrination is little more than parroting, motivated by fear of the group in control. Right thinking and integrity, motivated by God's love, are really what we are after. And to arrive at that, churches need to provide opportunities in which it is safe to ask questions, settings in which it is safe to be a little off at first, without being condemned for honestly seeking truth. If it is true that God grants people a great amount of freedom, should the Church grant any less in its attempt to help people to Christian maturity? Should it not grant just as much freedom, laying the solid foundation which is the character of God, by which we may appraise ideas in the world?

Education, not indoctrination, is the work of the Church, to be carried out in a spirit of deep humility.

KEEPERS

A couple days before my father passed away, my mom, my sister, my brother and a few of our adult children prepared to sit down for dinner at my parents' dining room table. It was the same table my parents owned all the years that I can remember—sturdy, made of oak, with seating for eight. My father's place had always been at the head. That night my mother told me to sit at the head. "You will soon be the patriarch of the family," she said. "You sit there." So I did.

She didn't see the lump in my throat. It was an honor to sit there. But it was a weight upon me too. When my father went to be with Jesus, it became my responsibility to care for the rest of the family. I was required to be wise, to be balanced, to give sound counsel, to know things others need to know, to encourage healthy risk-taking, to warn of impending danger, to provide a safety net when I could; also to allow others the freedom to make mistakes, to foster hope and joy and faith and peace and love and grace. I was likewise required not to be heavy-handed, short-sighted, argumentative, authoritarian or foolish. I hoped that I could be all I should be, and avoid all that I should avoid.

I have thought several times since that night of God's conversation with Cain after Cain killed Abel.

The Lord asked, "Where is your brother Abel?" Cain retorted (lying as he did so), "I don't know. Am I my brother's keeper?" The truth was that God *did* expect him to be his brother's keeper. We are all expected to be "keepers" of our brothers and sisters and mothers and fathers, as they have need and we have strength and the ability to meet their needs. That is how God's family works.

Not everyone likes "keeping," and not everyone likes being "kept." Much depends upon the spirit and motives of the keeping. But when the spirit is good and the motives are pure, there is a wonderful sturdiness to the family.

I decided that I would do all right in my "keeping," in my role as patriarch, if I could remember three things, the same three I try to remember in ministry: Listen to the people, then listen to God, and don't take myself too seriously.

LAMININ

Sometimes the Bible is more literally true than we realize.

In Colossians 1:16-17 we read, "For by Him [Jesus] all things were created: things in heaven and things on earth, visible and invisible, whether thrones or powers or rulers or authorities; all things were created by Him and for Him. He is before all things, and *in Him all things hold together...* " [emphasis mine].

There is a cell adhesion molecule called laminin. It is a specialized protein that acts as a kind of glue holding the cells together in the human body. In fact, all living things which have proteins have laminin. To use a different word picture, it is the rebar of the cell world. It holds things together the way rebar holds concrete together.

The shape of the laminin molecule is the reason it is significant. You need an electron microscope to see it, but it is unmistakably the work of God and proclaims the truth of the verses found in Colossians. Laminin looks like the *cross* on which Jesus died.

By His sacrificial love He really does hold all things together.

LETTER TO MY YOUNGER SON

(This letter was written in April of 2010 after a not-so-great morning. My younger son was 16, a sophomore at Proctor High School. He saved this letter, and it is used here with his permission.)

Dear Jackson,

I am very sorry for the way I talked to you this morning. Even if some of the things were on target and important, I did not find the right way to talk with you. You are a young man of intelligence and of a sensitive spirit, and I should have found a different and better way to talk with you.

We live in a world drifting away from God, and sometimes I am afraid our family will drift away too. It is not good to be afraid in this way. It is much better to have faith and to ask God for help and to talk things over, but sometimes fear is stronger than faith in me. That is something I must work on, and perhaps God will use you to help me with it.

I want you to be sharp and to recognize when something ungodly is on TV or in a book. I am trying to teach these things because the world teaches that almost everything is okay, and that there is no danger of drifting away from God. But God's ways have always been different enough from the ways of the world that people notice the difference. And the world makes fun of Christians and tries to get them to be like everybody else—watching and reading and doing and saying what everybody else watches and reads and does and says.

The Bible says that one of the marks of a mature Christian is that he or she can tell the difference between right and wrong. Right is always based on God's character. Wrong is based on the character of God's Enemy, who tries very hard to make wrong things look good ... or harmless. Usually we find out we are in trouble *after* we are already in it. *After* the relationship with God or another person has been damaged.

I hope your relationship with God will always be strong and healthy. And that your relationship with mom and me will also be strong and healthy and full of love. As you move into manhood, I will try to use *encouragement*, not anger to guide you. Please pray for me to do this well.

Love,
Dad

LIGHTING THE DUMPSTER ON FIRE

Not everyone knows it, but I lit the church dumpster on fire. Not on purpose of course. It was like this: After the Annual Sunday School Picnic to recognize all of our teachers and workers, the charcoal grills outside the back door had been left to cool. They cooled for a day and I checked them. There were still a few hot embers, so I let them cool some more. The next day I was sure the coals were out and I tossed them into the dumpster.

Coals can remain hot a long time under ashes, and these coals were not cool yet. The next day I went to throw something into the dumpster and found it had been the site of a fire. Fortunately the dumpster is made of steel and wasn't damaged. But the plastic lids on top melted a bit. They are now replaced.

Feeling pretty foolish, I confessed my sin to the trustees and to the garbage company. Both understood and forgave. Who would have thought the coals would smolder so long?

Sometimes there is something smoldering in our lives, too: anger, unwillingness to forgive, a grudge we bear. Perhaps you have heard the proverb that holding a grudge is like drinking poison and expecting the other person to die. It doesn't work that way. Unresolved anger burns those who carry it around with them just like the fire burned the dumpster that held the coals.

In their book, *True Faced*, a take-off on the phrase "two-faced," Bill Thrall, Bruce McNicol and John Lynch urge that Christians resolve as many conflicts as possible, so as to live true to Jesus and to avoid fires inside that burn all their relationships. This is not easy work, and sometimes we go about it in an ineffective way.

One thing that hinders us is attempting to forgive a person when we have not admitted our hurt to God first. We can, however, take that first step: Confess our injury to God and ask Him to give us His spirit of mercy. It isn't all that needs to be done, but it is a start. It's that or smolder some more until a fire breaks out.

MORE THAN ANYONE BARGAINS FOR

R.C. Sproul said that it is hard to explain the concept of holiness. He noted in his book, *The Holiness of God*, that it took three chapters to work up to some kind of definition of it. The Hebrew word from which it derives means "to cut." We might think of holiness as a cut above—infinitely above—everything else. It contains within it the idea of purity, but it is much more than that. It means "foreign" or "alien" to common experience, and so is something at once frightening and exhilarating.

To encounter holiness is to be in awe. A friend of mine once explained awe in this way: suppose you were flying off the coast of California in a helicopter and you were dropped into the ocean next to a blue whale, which is enormous and could swallow you, but is also gentle and probably would not. You would likely experience awe. I think this is what the close friends of Jesus felt on the day they encountered Him, recently risen from the dead.

Some women went to the tomb early in the morning, just as the sun was rising, wondering how they would roll the heavy, circular stone away from the door. To their surprise it was already rolled away, and a young man dressed in a white robe sat inside the tomb. He showed them the place where Jesus had been laid after being crucified. The angel—for that is what he was—told them that Jesus had risen from the dead. The women fled the grave, trembling and amazed, frightened and exhilarated after an encounter with holiness. They were supposed to tell Jesus' disciples what had happened, but the narrative says "they said nothing to nobody, because they were terrified." (The Greek text uses a double negative to make a point.)

The same thing kept occurring all day long. It happened to Peter and John, then to Mary Magdalene, then to two men on the road to a town called Emmaus, and finally to the group of disciples that evening behind locked doors in Jerusalem. As Peter and John looked at dawn into the empty tomb and put two and two together; and as Mary and the two on the road saw Jesus Himself, but did not immediately recognize Him; and as the disciples behind locked doors saw the nail prints in His hands and feet and saw where the spear of the Roman soldier had pierced His side, they all encountered something so completely different than anything they had ever encountered before: the holiness of God up close and personal.

Our God-talk is full of love and often justice (or judgment, depending upon the conversation), but not more than half-full of holiness. Perhaps that should change. I remember a night at Mission Meadows Covenant Bible Camp in Dewittville, New York when I was eleven years old. That night I encountered Jesus in His holiness. It was a frightening and exhilarating experience: Frightening, because I knew that I was sinful in comparison to Him and deserved to lose my life; exhilarating, because I also knew that, in His kindness, Jesus heard my admission of guilt, forgave me completely, and was beginning to make me into a new person. I might have been "swallowed" by His enormity, but I found Him to be gentle. His love overcame the fear that I felt.

Not everyone has exactly the same experience when they meet Jesus. But at some point in time, in a relationship with Him, holiness is encountered. There comes a moment when we say, as did the disciples right after Jesus stilled a storm, "Who *is* this?" And we wonder: Will He kill me with His holiness or save me with His kindness? Job, who had so many troubles that they became proverbial, once said, "Even though He slay me, I will hope in Him" (Job 13:15). If I have faith—that is, if I put my life into His hands to use as He sees fit—the answer is: He will save me. He will save me from my sin because He paid for it on the cross. He will save me from death because He conquered death and can share that power to live again after dying. His holiness next to my un-holiness is how I know I need Him. His holiness is more than anyone bargains for.

But so is His goodness.

ODYSSEY

Matt is on an odyssey ... from Abilene, Texas to Virginia, Minnesota.

Why isn't exactly clear. He says there is a man named John in Virginia who has construction work for him. But who has construction projects on the Iron Range in winter? And why does a man from the warm south come this far north for such a job?

Matt never knew his father. His mother died last year in Texas, of cancer. He is an only child and a thirty-three year old orphan. He is eager to help with our church building project and rolls white paint in the stairwell leading to the basement. He is equal parts overconfident and unskilled in his work. He takes frequent smoke breaks. He is a champion at burping. He wears ill-fitting black wind pants, a blue fleece-lined hooded sweatshirt, a black stocking cap and black casual shoes. When he drops the paint roller on his shoe, he does not wipe the paint off. Now the shoe has character, he says. Among his effects, strewn on the floor by the elevator, are a blaze-orange jacket and a green bedspread.

Matt knows the Bible. This emerges as a gradual revelation to me. He is disdainful of preachers who drive Cadillacs. (I have looked at Cadillacs, but am glad I own an eleven year old Subaru with 190,000 miles.) He asks questions and seems willing to learn. Sometimes he asks a new question before getting an answer to the last one. Life has been hard for him. I tell him about a loving heavenly Father and the Son who paid a ransom for all men. He is interested but non-committal.

One of the trustees has offered to let him spend the night in the church. It is going to be close to zero degrees outside. I stay overnight in the church too, in order to talk. In order to see what his uncertain world is like. For several hours Matt drinks coffee and reads the Bible. I work on my sermon.

About midnight Matt confesses that there is no job waiting in Virginia. He also confesses to having served time for assault. Though Matt is respectful and I don't feel afraid, I am glad he is staying in the church and not in someone's home. There are both light and poignant moments in our conversation.

I fall asleep on a string of chairs in the sanctuary. I leave the couch for Matt. I leave a blanket from my car for him too. My jacket is my blanket, but at sixty degrees, it is not enough. I am cold most of the night. Matt never comes to sleep. He reads. He makes popcorn. He drinks coffee.

In the morning we make pancakes. Matt is eager but not especially skilled. The first pancake is so thick it doesn't bake properly. A carpenter and two carpet layers working on the church join us for breakfast. We eat standing around the island in the kitchen. We listen to Minnesota Public Radio and the talk is mostly of the stock market. The pancakes are much better than the economy.

Matt wants a pair of pants. His wind pants keep dropping below the equator. We talk about going to Goodwill just down the road. I have $3.50, but there is some petty cash at church, enough to buy Matt an entire set of clothes at Goodwill. We talk about going to a shelter or the new men's residence that has just opened up. We talk about staying in Duluth where there might be more job opportunities. Matt is reluctant. It becomes clear that he wants me to drive him to Virginia, which I cannot do because of other obligations.

Suddenly everything changes. Matt no longer wants clothes, not even pants. He just wants to go to Virginia. I take him to the Holiday station at Midway Road and Highway 53. He leaves with few words, wearing my gloves and carrying a Bible he has claimed from the church. As I head off to the Douglas County Jail in Superior, Wisconsin to visit inmates, I see Matt walking the road toward Virginia. I pray that he doesn't freeze. He has no socks. My time with Matt has not ended well. He has freedom and direction, but no home or job, no family or church.

I am launched on an odyssey to discern truth from manipulative story, to find a way to be of real help to the next Matt who crosses my path.

PARADOXES

Some things only make sense when they make no sense at all. I know that sounds foolish, but it isn't. And we have a word for this phenomenon: We call it a paradox. Perhaps I can illustrate with Pagan and Christian virtues.

G.K. Chesterton, in his book *Heretics*, describes what he says are two pagan virtues: justice and temperance. (By way of clarification, Paganism for Chesterton is not the absence of religion, but the essence of religion before Christianity became known to the world.) Cultures and religions have varied in their application of these virtues, but they certainly were around before Christianity became widely known. Justice, he says, "consists in finding out a certain thing due to a certain man and giving it to him." And temperance "consists in finding out the proper limit of a particular indulgence and adhering to that." The definitions are easy to understand. They make sense. And the behaviors of persons administering justice, or restraining themselves by temperance, are sensible too.

By contrast, some Christian virtues make no sense at all. Consider the three Christian virtues of charity, hope and faith. According to Chesterton, charity "means pardoning what is unpardonable ... hope means hoping when things are hopeless . . . and faith means believing the incredible." The definitions defy logic, and so does the behavior of persons engaged in these virtues. And yet, it cannot be otherwise. The definitions are correct and the behaviors of people engaged in charity, hope and faith are accurately put forth. Such paradoxes set Christianity apart from Paganism. And although Paganism has claimed its share of mystery, not much is more mysterious than these paradoxical Christian virtues.

Some say that Christian faith is "the power of believing that which we know to be untrue." But truth is often strange, and because of its strangeness, assumed to be untrue. It would be better to say that Christian faith is belief in truths that are sometimes paradoxical.

General truth is sometimes paradoxical too. Take two examples from the physical world. Almost everything contracts as it gets colder. But water does not obey the rule. When it freezes it expands, which is why expansion joints are needed on bridges and in concrete sidewalks. Also, as a general principle, denser objects sink in less dense liquids. But because of buoyancy, huge steel ships, much denser than water, contradict the principle and float. Since there are believable paradoxes in the natural world, why not assume paradoxes in the supernatural world? Is it more difficult to believe the Incarnation—God and man in the same frame—than to believe that water expands when it freezes? Or is it more difficult to believe the baffling aspects of the Trinity—three persons, yet one God—than to believe that steel ships float on water?

My North Park Theological Seminary New Testament professor once said that truth often comes anchored in seeming contradictions, like a guitar string anchored at two different points. If there were only one fixed "point of truth," there would be no vibration of the string, no music. Sometimes you need two seemingly contradictory truths to make the full truth, and the music of life.

The Christian Faith does not require believing what is untrue, as some suppose, but rather believing seemingly contradictory truths which make up a fuller truth. Even those who do not embrace Christianity understand and live with the Christian paradoxes of charity, hope and faith. It is not a large leap from such paradoxes to others describing the Incarnation or the Trinity or the Virgin Birth or the Resurrection of Jesus from the dead.

Christianity is not unbelievable; it is just wonderfully mysterious.

PAROUSIA

I pulled my Subaru wagon onto the apron at the corner of Observation and Skyline Drives. It was Wednesday, May 14, 2008 and the Snowbird aerial performers were scheduled to appear over the Duluth, Minnesota harbor at 4:15 pm. I had arrived a little early to get a good spot, and as the time for the show approached, more cars joined mine at the scenic overlook.

The appointed time came and went. I strained to see the harbor. I scanned the horizon. I listened for the drone of engines. Nothing. The gal to my left got some shelled peanuts from the back of her SUV. The fellow in the passenger car to my right started wondering where the nearest restroom might be. A few people left altogether.

I checked my information. The paper said 4:15 pm. I waited longer. The gal in the SUV had the radio on, and the announcer was talking about the air show. New information: The crew was taking off at 5:15 pm from Duluth International and would appear at 5:30 pm. I checked my watch. It was five o'clock. I had just enough time.

I backed my car out and turned toward Proctor. If traffic was not bad I could make it home in time to pick up my younger son, swing back, catch some of the show and still make it to his youth group and my Bible Study by six o'clock.

As I passed the railroad yard in Proctor, I could see the CT-114s in silhouette over the roundhouse. I reached the driveway, my son hopped in, and we were off again. Down Thompson Hill we sped, past the paper mill, streaming by the ore docks, eyes riveted on the lift bridge. Off at 21st Avenue West, up Highway 53. At Piedmont Avenue, Jackson saw them: nine beautiful birds of steel, white on top, orange underneath. Climbing, diving, leveling off in perfect formation. They rose like a fountain, opened like a flower and curled under, trailing their white smoke, then rose again to explode into the sky like fireworks.

Christians have an aerial show they are waiting for. It is called the parousia. The word means "appearing." It is the appearing of Jesus in the air that we are straining to see. Like the newspaper giving the time of the Snowbird performance, the Old Testament has given a general idea of the expected time of Christ's arrival. Like the radio broadcast, the New Testament has refined the timetable. Like the folks who left the scenic overlook, some people become impatient waiting for Jesus, or figure He is not going to come. But He is coming, and if what I have been reading lately is accurate, it will not be long.

On May 15, 2008 Israel celebrated sixty years as a nation. The re-establishment of Israel is the single most significant indicator that the parousia is near. 2,700 years ago Isaiah prophesied that this would happen (Isaiah 66:7-8). There are other indicators such as wars, natural disasters, and social and political upheavals which we now observe in the world. Jesus spoke about these things in Matthew 24. The Bible says that when things become very bad, people who have trusted in Jesus will be rescued, but those who have not will experience tragedy. So what people do between now and then is terribly important. At some juncture there will be no time left to change course, change character or make a different decision about how to live.

It has always been God's way to let people know what He is doing. And to delay a while to give folks time to respond to His kindness and ask to be rescued from sin. But He will not wait forever. Some people are suffering greatly already, and He wants to stop their suffering and make right what has been wrong and unfair. Things will be put right when Jesus comes. For those who love Him, who are watching, the appearance of Jesus will be welcome and thrilling (imagine life suddenly becoming really good and then going on that way forever). But for those who are indifferent or who have dismissed Him, it will be an occasion of sudden understanding and deep regret.

There is a choice to be made.

RAILROADING
AND SANDBAGGING

Someday I am going to invent a really good Christmas tree stand. It will not be like the plastic or metal stands available now. It won't require a plywood base to keep things level and steady. It will be solid. It will have a wide base, a tall open cylinder for the tree and a plastic insert for the water. There will be easily adjustable bolts. If the trunk is thick or thin, it will work. If the tree is straight or bent, it will work.

I am resolved to do this because one year we picked out a tree that was straight not-so-much. It looked straight at the lot, but about two feet up the trunk, the tree took off at a sharp angle and aimed itself toward Nebraska. I wanted to cut the trunk off, but my wife said, "We have this conversation every year." And, "You'll figure something out."

The tree went up. My fingers were sore from cranking on those little L-bolts that did eventually make the tree straight. But that did not keep the tree from wanting to tip over. What I figured out was to lay a length of railroad track on the base of the stand (buying a home from a railroad man is a plus in situations like this) and I fortified same with a pillowcase filled with sand. The tree skirt over this weighty solution had a big hump, but the tree did not tip over. When you looked at the tree from another room, and the door between you and the tree was closed, it looked pretty good.

Life is often not what we expect. What seems straight often turns out to be bent. And our efforts to make circumstances and relationships come out right, or at least better, leave us sore in both body and spirit. Even if we get things somewhat upright, life threatens to tip over on us. It is then that the simple act of prayer helps. In one of my devotions, I read Colossians 4:12: "Epaphras ... is always wrestling in prayer for you, that you may stand firm in all the will of God, mature and fully assured." By God's wonderful arrangement, prayer helps us to stand firm. Prayer helps us to be mature. Prayer helps us to be fully assured. Not wave-and-smile prayers, mind you, but wrestling prayers that take a little time, effort, strategy and persistence. There isn't any particular formula for this; you just do it and get better as you go.

You can rail and sandbag your life, like I did my Christmas tree. You can make do with odd contraptions and conniptions. But prayer is a much better way to keep life from tipping over.

SCOPE FOR IMAGINATION

I put a rifle scope on my Browning lever action one year before the start of deer season. It was the first scope I owned. I bought it used at our church garage sale for ten dollars. It was a 2.5x10x40 Bushnell. I didn't know what all the numbers meant until I got the scope. A salesman at Gander Mountain explained them to me. Things in the scope will appear 2.5 times to 10 times larger, as you twist the ring on the barrel of the scope, than what your eye can see alone, and the "eye" of the scope is 40 millimeters in diameter. Practically speaking, my fifty-plus year-old blurry peeper could now see clearly what it was shooting at when the target was far away.

 I already had bases on which to mount the scope to the rifle. Mine were the Weaver style, three dimensional trapezoids that screw into the top of the rifle receiver. I needed rings, so I went to Fisherman's Corner and picked up some Leupold side-by-sides. Rings are either top and bottom sections or side-by-side sections, held together by screws that grip the scope in a kind of round clamp. When you get it all together—scope inside rings on bases on rifle—the scope has to be at least three inches from your eye as you are shooting. If your eye is closer, the kick of the rifle blows the scope back into your eye and your favorite colors are black and purple for a couple weeks. I once borrowed a Winchester .30/.30 with a scope (before I bought my own rifle) and I wore those colors after a practice shot. Some scopes come with rubber cushions, because some hunters are slow learners.

Sighting in is the next step. Just because you have a scope and can see things clearly doesn't mean you can hit what you aim to shoot. Most scopes have two dials, one to adjust left and right, one to adjust up and down. You turn each dial all the way to one side, then all the way to the other side, taking note the second time how many circuits the dial makes. Then you figure out what half of that is and return to it. Hopefully, when you begin to shoot real bullets, they land somewhere "on the paper," which is to say, the target. It helps to start out at a distance of only twenty-five yards. And it bolsters confidence. Sighting in is best done from a bench rest, i.e. a table with a sandbag on it, to steady the front of the rifle. Unless you have ice water in your veins, the barrel of the rifle wanders a bit when you hold it freehand. Fine tuning the dials completes the process. The dials make an audible "click" each time there is a tiny adjustment causing the bullet to hit a quarter inch more toward where you want than it did last time. The goal is to shoot three bullets into the same spot right in the center of the target at a distance of twenty five yards, and have a small spread at one hundred yards. The sighting in distance may be longer if you shoot out west where deer and elk do not like to be that near to you.

I hoped the scope would be of real benefit. I did get a deer without one the previous year. And to be honest, I did not know if I liked the scope. It changed the weight and feel of the rifle, which were just about perfect. Change is hard for all of us.

This put me in mind of one change we really must make, if we are to live well. When the close friends of Jesus were arguing over which of them was the greatest, He called a little child and had him stand among them. "I tell you the truth," He said, "unless you change and become like little children, you will never enter the kingdom of heaven" (Matthew 18:3). He meant, I believe, to become humble, knowing you are not self-sufficient, but in need of a Savior. And to become trusting, like a child, who figures there will always be a peanut butter sandwich when he needs it. An admonition to become childlike was probably not what coarse fishermen expected to hear. But they made the change. Except for the one who betrayed Him, they trusted in Jesus for forgiveness and for provision.

It opened up some scope for imagination for Jesus' disciples. It sharpened their focus. They hit the target in life. So do all of us who make the same change.

SHE TOUCHED A PEACH

My wife and I were picking up a few groceries at the Super One in West Duluth, Minnesota when the checkout clerk suddenly looked up alarmed, said she had to wash her hands and dashed to the rest room. Standing at the end of the belt where I was bagging, I had missed the emergency. "She touched a peach," my wife explained, "and she is very allergic to them."

When the clerk returned she mentioned that just touching that particular fruit causes her to break out in a bad rash up and down her arm. She couldn't afford that right now as she was training for an Iron Man competition. The Iron Man is a triathlon requiring swimming, biking and running. It is grueling and meant for serious athletes.

It occurs to me that Christians ought to take the same approach toward sin that the clerk took toward peaches. What if we were constantly vigilant instead of passively tolerant of sin? What if, when inadvertently "touching" sin, we dashed off to confession and washed our hands of the offense? Might we be better able to "compete" in some of life's more grueling and serious events? How often do we end up on the injured or inactive list with some kind of "rash" we could have avoided?

Peaches aren't always toxic. But sin is. It is best not to touch it at all. But if we do, we have help in confession that washes the toxin away.

SHOULD WE LEGALIZE SAME SEX MARRIAGES?

An editorial in the *Duluth News-Tribune* suggested that, as a nation, we should legalize same sex marriages. Some states have already done so. While we are considering such an action, we might want to ask a few important questions.

One is, if we do this, what else changes besides the law? R.C. Sproul, an American theologian, says that over time we are becoming a society which looks to morals rather than to ethics to decide what to do and how to live. While these two may seem to be roughly the same, they are significantly different. The word "morals" comes from "mores" which are the customs by which a society lives. Ethics, on the other hand, are principles based on a standard of right and wrong. Morals are chosen by consensus; ethics by measuring behavior against a standard that does not change and so is always reliable. Sproul says that in America we are starting to live by a "statistical morality," which means that we take a poll, see what people think, and go with the majority, or in some cases, with the most vocal minority. Right and wrong do not need to enter the picture. What matters is that we find a consensus. Many newspapers and news shows now invite their audiences to weigh in on issues of the day. What is being sought is a consensus on events and the decisions made by others, and the popular opinion becomes the rule by which we live.

This works fine if people are basically good. But another question we might ask is, are people basically good? Del Tackett, the host of The Truth Project [www.thetruthproject.org] suggests that people are not basically good. If they are, he asks, how do you account for evil in the world? Some worldviews account for it by saying that *people* are basically good, and evil is the result of a malfunction in *society*. But, Tackett asks, since a society is made up of people, isn't evil still traceable to people? And if people are the cause of injustice, abuses of power, inequality, poverty, war and so forth, is statistical morality such a good way to decide how we are going to live? All worldviews make claims to "truth" and the claims are supposed to reflect how things really are. That people are basically good is a truth claim in a worldview called humanism. But maybe that is not how it really is. If we change the law regarding same sex marriages, might we end up with a rule for living based on the majority opinion (or vocal minority opinion) of people who are basically flawed? suppose it is not comfortable to call ourselves flawed but it does reflect our reality.

Several years ago, I visited with a Unitarian Universalist pastor and we were discussing the issue of homosexuality. She brought with her a manual produced by her denomination to assist in the process which would result in the legalization of same sex marriages. In the manual was the suggestion to turn every discussion away from right and wrong and make it about civil rights. It is true that gay people have been wrongly treated, and this should stop. But the suggestion in the manual reveals an intentional shift away from ethics and away from an unchanging, reliable standard. The question of right and wrong is simply bypassed. Or, right and wrong are defined in a new way that now permits a behavior once considered to be wrong. Do we want to do that? Will we lose something important if we change our definitions? In a truly just society should not *both* ethics and civil rights be observed?

A Lutheran colleague of mine puts it even more pointedly. He says if we are now going to say that homosexuality and same sex marriages are okay, we have to account for taking some things which have been in the category of "sin" for many centuries, and moving them into the category of "not sin." By what authority do we do that? If mankind is its own god, I suppose we could do that. The "truth" claim of humanism is that we *are* our own gods. But humanism also says that people are basically good, and that does not reflect reality. In fact, people make very poor gods. Perhaps another worldview would be helpful. Perhaps a standard outside humanity would be better when considering our behavior, before legalizing what has been illegal since laws were first set down.

Perhaps we should think about this a little more.

SNOW ANGELS

On the heels of deer season one November, as a part of a Sustaining Pastoral Excellence Program, I had a chance to do a prayer and solitude retreat at the Adventurous Christians Wilderness Center in the Boundary Waters of northern Minnesota. AC, as most people call it, is easy to reach. You travel north to Grand Marais, turn left onto the Gunflint trail and go thirty-five miles until you see the sign by the driveway. I had the run of two rooms in a one hundred year-old cabin, wonderful and healthy meals, and attention from Sally, the sled dog. It was a time of great refreshment. There was uninterrupted time with God, time for reflection, time to read God's Word, time to rest. And for diversion, I was invited by my host to go cross-country skiing one afternoon.

The sky was overcast, but not bleak, the air brisk, but not icy. I had taken a variety of outdoor clothes, so I donned a wool shirt and a windbreaker, a baseball cap and wool gloves.

Cross-country skiing has changed since I last tried it. In the lodge at AC, hanging on a wall, there are a pair of long, wide spruce skis, such as were used by long, wide Norwegians. These are the skis I remember having used before. Now the skis are narrow, and people do this thing called "skate skiing" which looks like Olympic ice skating, only on skis, on a trail in the woods.

As it turns out, I am a natural, but not at cross-country skiing. After an initial run of fifty yards, I suddenly and inexplicably felt a need to test gravity. It still works. This was followed by a chance to examine the fresh powder on the ground very close up. Same stuff we have here, pretty much. We went on a ways, and every so often, my friend Russ would stop and let me catch up, or give me a pointer about how to move a leg with an opposite arm or use a pole more effectively. We found a good place to turn around and regained the pickup truck before sunset.

On the way back I observed the record of my progress: a modest attempt at skate skiing, then a snow angel; a nice snowplow configuration at the top of a hill, then a snow angel; skis following in the tracks Russ made, then a snow angel.

It occurred to me that our progress in the Christian life is much the same. There are moments when we shine, when we are fluid, intuitive, graceful. We glide and have the luxury of looking around at the scenery, feel like we belong in our surroundings, have hearts filled with joy, value the service we are able to render to God, love all of humanity, and glow with assurance. And then there are other moments, recorded like angels in the snow, marking the places we lost balance, forgot what we were doing, tested gravity, worked hard only to spill onto the trail, maybe into a ravine or onto a sharp rock.

As I considered the snow angels I had made on the trail that November afternoon, I wondered what God thinks about my progress in the Christian life. No doubt there are times when He is grieved that I am not further along and more like Him in character and behavior. I imagine there are also times when my progress, tortured as it may be, is still progress, and gives Him pleasure. Sometimes, when the slipping is not sinful, just weird in judgment and acrobatic in a clown kind of way, perhaps He laughs out loud.

I discovered a verse while on the prayer and solitude retreat, one that continues to guide me. It is from Hebrews 6:1 and says, "Therefore let us move beyond the elementary teachings about Christ and be taken forward to maturity ..." We cannot gain spiritual maturity without some mistakes. It is worth the effort, however, in the same way that a novice finds it worth the effort to become a proficient skier. We are not meant to remain novices in our faith, but to grow into maturity, becoming wise, strong and adventurous. If we do not lose heart, we will get there. Like my friend, Russ, God pauses on the trail to let us catch up. He gives us pointers in His Word and through His Spirit. He is more eager for our success than we are. There are exciting slopes and landscapes not everyone sees that He wants to share with us.

And the snow angels? Actual or spiritual, they are part of the journey to maturity.

SOME COMMON SENSE ABOUT ANGER

We all have ideas about anger, but not all the ideas come from a source of wisdom. I've made a study of anger, experimenting with passive-aggressive and plain aggressive forms. I have smoldered, begrudged, lit a short fuse, let the fuse burn a good long while, plotted mental revenge, acted pitiful, gone to counseling, given counsel, exploded and imploded, burned others and burned myself with a hot flame, listened to God's Spirit and looked into God's Word, and I've come to a few conclusions about anger.

Conclusion #1: All anger is not bad. If it were, God's Word would tell us never to be angry. But in fact the Bible anticipates that we will be angry at times. Psalm 4:4 gives this advice: "In your anger do not sin." A counselor once told me that as long as I do not hurt myself or hurt others or destroy property, I am doing all right with anger.

Conclusion #2: Other people do not make us angry. The truth is that we choose whether or not to get angry. It is natural to blame others, and it gets us off the hook, but our anger is of our own making. When Cain was angry with his brother, Abel, for having a sacrifice more acceptable to God, the LORD said to Cain, "... sin is crouching at the door; it desires to have you, but you must master it." If it is possible to master the sinful kind of anger, we should not blame others for it. Cain did not master his anger and he became the world's first murderer.

Conclusion #3: Blowing up occasionally, while understandable, is not excusable. Blowing up usually has a verbal component to it, which is to say that some words escape our lips that are pretty high powered. Proverbs 18:21 reminds us that "the tongue has the power of life and death." We can harm with our words as well as with a fist or a stick. Blowing off steam with physical activity may be helpful, but blowing up and injuring someone else's spirit never is. Words can be strong without being destructive. If the strong words we know are all destructive, we may need to learn some new words.

Conclusion #4: Anger requires some kind of action. We may think that we are doing ourselves and others a favor by not acting on our anger, but that is not true. Anger can be a good motivator to act and change something that is not working. When we do not act, we are likely to become passive-aggressive, which is very unkind to others, or to become depressed, which is very unkind to ourselves. Ephesians 4:26 urges, "Do not let the sun go down on your anger." In other words, try to act on it in a timely fashion. Stating how we feel or naming the cause (e.g. a person's behavior, which is not the same as blaming the person) can be of great benefit.

Conclusion #5: There is a purpose for anger. God gave anger to human beings as a tool, with a good purpose: to stand up to evil. Jesus was standing up to evil when He cleared the temple of moneychangers and merchants in Mark 11:12-18. They were cheating people and denying the Gentiles a place to worship. Revenge is not the purpose. Bending others to our will is not the purpose. Catharsis is not the purpose. Fighting for the poor, the disenfranchised, the weak, the helpless and the hopeless, is the reason we have the tool.

This does not exhaust the topic of anger. But it is a starting point for making some corrections. In my study of anger I have found that it is wiser to correct myself rather than to try to correct others. Because when I correct others, it only makes them angry.

SQUIRREL OR CHIPMUNK?

I was walking down a logging road on a Sunday afternoon in October on the county land where I hunt. With me were my partners and a new fellow who was hunting the area that year. Ostensibly we were checking our stands, picking a place for the new guy, checking the location of trails and the size of tracks, repairing one blind, and establishing a protocol for filling our tags. Actually, I think we were just out for a pleasant hike, breathing in the smell of fall leaves, enjoying the changing colors, and reveling in the friendship we have. We were reveling also in the chance to relive some great moments. In our group the great moments usually start with: "The buck stepped out of the forest. He stamped his foot and the earth shook. Lightning split the sky ..."

After making our rounds of the different stands, we headed into a cedar grove to check the last ground blind. It was quiet there, out of the wind, and peaceful, the more so because of light snow on the floor of the woods. We all stood still and listened to the silence. Then, from up in the trees, came a scolding trill. We listened hard. Pretty soon a lively debate ensued. Was it a bird? No, a squirrel. You don't mean a squirrel, you mean a chipmunk. No, a squirrel. Definitely *not* a squirrel! Definitely *not* a chipmunk! Yes, a chipmunk, tan with black stripes! But this was red or gray with a bushy tail, and larger than a chipmunk!

There were two main debaters, and several tag team members on each side, calling on all their accumulated wood lore and several unrelated authorities to aid the cause. It was decided the thing had to be sighted, which it was, but only fleetingly in the tangle of vines in the trees. And so I am not sure if there was a clear decision. The two main parties stayed in the cedar grove longer than the rest and came out friends, which is the best way for that kind of conversation to end.

In matters of faith we sometimes differ with each other, and the outcomes are not so amicable. At times our certainty about something, usually in Scripture, drives us to break fellowship with other members of the body of Christ who think differently. Not all differences can be resolved of course. Some people twist truth to make it say what they want. When that happens, understanding God's intentions and preserving any common ground are both lost. Jesus once told some religious leaders, "You have a fine way of setting aside the commands of God to observe your own traditions!" (Mark 7:9).

But many things are a matter of interpretation and not truth. And the fellowship remains sweet if we are of a mind to preserve it. Jesus told His followers, "Have salt in yourselves [a firm commitment to being My disciples], and be at peace with each other" (Mark 9:50). Our Lord has only one body, the parts of which He hopes will work together in peace to accomplish His purposes.

And for the record, it was a squirrel.

THE ANGRY WOMAN

When I first saw her, I was disturbed. She was looking straight back at me and she was disturbed too. I could see that she was angry and hurt. The woman was formulating some words that might well have been a tongue-lashing or a curse. I don't know. I didn't actually hear her speak. She is a woman in a painting. Not beautiful but not graceless either. She is hard-featured and expressive, perched on the edge of a bench, wearing a yellow sun dress. And though she is bound to the canvas, she is real enough and she haunts me.

My friend Nelson Anderson painted her. He is a pastor like me, but he is also a professional artist. Artists don't always tell you about their work. Maybe telling people blocks further inspiration. Maybe telling people reveals more of the artist than the artist wishes to reveal. Maybe telling people limits the capacity of the work to connect with the viewers and make an impact. But Nelson did tell me this about the angry woman: she might represent those people who are in great need, who look to the Church as a source of love and compassion, and who are turned away or ignored. When he told me this, immediately I could think of several people who have asked for help and were disappointed, because we have hoops to jump through. And because we don't want to be unwise in the use of God's resources. And because we don't want to be conned.

In fairness, almost none of the requests that come to the Church are easy to accommodate. A ragged man, a Vietnam vet who was homeless and jobless, came to the church I was serving in New Jersey some years ago. He wanted money so he could drink. When I didn't give him any, he looked at me with anger and hurt. He threatened suicide. His death, he said, would be on my head. I wasn't sure how to respond, but I prayed for him and God impressed on me a verse from His word: "Give to the one who asks you ..." (Matthew 5:42). Money didn't seem like the thing. What else did I have? The man was living in a tent on the edge of a golf course. It dawned on me that he might need camping equipment. I had a good pack on an aluminum frame. When he came back not dead, I breathed a sigh of relief and gave him the pack. He came back again and got a warm hat. The next time it was a pair of gloves. We sort of became friends who could talk about Jesus. And the look on his face changed.

In the painting of the angry woman, there is a child on the woman's lap, a child who isn't all there. That is because Nelson hasn't finished the painting yet. Artists paint when inspiration strikes and inspiration struck Nelson, but not fully. So he is waiting until it strikes again. Nelson didn't tell me about the child, but that ghostly form might be the Church. Like a child in the lap, the Church may turn out to be a comfort or a burden to hurting people.

Whether the Church brings compassion or disappointment to people is always a little uncertain. Compassion is in God's nature and is meant to be in the nature of those who represent Him. But He doesn't force it on His representatives any more than the sun forces a man to take off his coat on a warm day. Everyone has a choice about being tender. Though God is warm, some of us who represent Him just stay cold.

I don't like being haunted by paintings, but a haunting thing seems to be a good motivator. Since viewing the painting, I have tried to think creatively, to use discernment and to take risks. I can still think of some people who are angry and hurt. But I can also think of some whose faces are no longer so, who know the love of God because of the Church. Nelson's art has shaped my behavior because it reminded me to obey the word of God and to give to those who ask. Dietrich Bonhoeffer once said, "If the hungry man does not attain to faith, then the guilt falls on those who refused him bread." There is some kind of bread, I believe, which can be given to everyone who asks. There is some kind of comfort which can be given to every angry woman.

THE BACHELOR'S-BUTTON

My wife is always trying to find the best place for things, which is why we had to relocate the Bachelor's-button in the flower bed. It had been planted along the back edge and was starting to sneak under the front steps, and my wife was pretty sure it should be out where people could see it better. That makes sense because it looks like the fireworks of the plant world. It has a pink, spiked center, periwinkle petals shooting off from that, and cottony leaves that seem to lift the flower head into the air and encourage it to explode.

So I got the shovel and dug carefully under it, trying to get all the roots and enough dirt to make it feel like it was still in its familiar place. I put it in a new hole in the center of the bed and tamped the earth around it. Half an hour later alarm bells were going off in my head because the prized flower was wilting. "We'd better get some water to this," I said to my wife.

"We will," she replied. "It will be fine."

"It doesn't look fine," I offered.

"They all do that," she remarked.

"I think it's dying," I said.

"It's not dying," she rejoined. "It will perk up."

But when evening shadows fell it was un-perked, despite having been watered and encouraged with words.

I went to bed feeling a little like King Darius who had been tricked into throwing Daniel into the lions' den. The king worried over Daniel that night and I worried over the plant. In the morning the king rushed to the lion's den to see if Daniel had survived, and I hurried out onto the front porch and looked over the railing to see if the Bachelor's-button had bitten the dust. Daniel survived the lions, and the Bachelor's-button survived the transplant. In fact, it looked quite healthy, as if it had been thriving in that spot all along.

I learned two things. One is that my wife knows more about plants than I do. The other is that God takes care of His stuff, and makes what He creates to be pretty resilient. This gives me hope for the times when God thinks I might do better somewhere else than where I have been, and some kind of change is in order. None of us likes change too much, and especially we do not like to change our thinking. It is a stretch to move to another "location" on a spiritual map where the terrain is unfamiliar or is not what we were taught, but upon investigation is biblical. Who hasn't learned about God's love, say, and just when that feels good and comfortable, discovered with some distress that God is also just and doesn't suffer fools well? Both things are true and both are on the spiritual map, but in different places.

In our life of faith we try to get our minds and hearts around the whole truth without becoming schizophrenic in the process. God makes us resilient so that we can survive the transplant. He knows we will do better if moved out from under the porch of partial truth toward which we have been sneaking.

To get us "transplanted" He uses two shovels. One is the Bible which, if we read the whole thing and not just selected parts, gives us the whole truth. The other is people who are not exactly like us but who are still recognizable as solid Christians. They know what we don't know and challenge us to get a bigger picture. As for wilting, I think it is just part of the process of being transplanted. We grieve when we leave what we have cherished. And for a while we don't look or feel too good. But God waters us with His Spirit and encourages us with His words and we perk up and begin to fulfill a better purpose.

And some of us find out we can shoot off some great and colorful spiritual fireworks.

THE CHALLENGE OF BEING TEACHABLE

When you find out that a certain part of the Old Testament is known as the LAW, do you chafe a bit? Do you still chafe when you find out that an equally good translation of LAW is "instruction"?

Many of us are less than thrilled at the thought of someone instructing us, even when it is God Himself. We do not say that out loud, of course, because then we would sound rather un-Christian. We recognize the need for discipline and correction in life and faith, but we do not like it much, even when it is kindly done. And we would be happier, I think, if we could choose the source of the correction when the source is another person. Instead, we find ourselves in a rock tumbler, disguised as a church, bumping against all our least favorite stones, getting the rough edges smoothed off, and taking on a polish that is "for our own good," but hard on the ego.

In 1973, *Life Magazine* put out a special issue marking the twenty-fifth anniversary of Israel as a modern nation. One article featured the Sabras—the "points of the sword"— young, energetic men in their twenties who held the promise of the re-established

Promised Land. They were respectful of the previous generation which had fought the Arabs to found their country. They themselves were fighters in the 1967 Seven Days War against Egypt that made Israel the dominant power in the Middle East. The Sabras had a swagger and confidence that many appreciated, but which left them not altogether teachable. Yoram Kaniuk, an Israeli-born novelist and journalist, writing about the character of the Sabra said, "He has learned that even when he isn't right, others are right even less." Does it seem to you that we often live out our Christian lives with the same attitude, thinking that though we are not always right, others are right even less?

It is a curse constantly to second guess yourself. I know that from personal experience. But it is also a curse to be un-teachable. The entire Book of Proverbs is aimed toward teaching young people (and the young at heart) how to live well before God. The first instruction is to have a deep reverence, sometimes called "fear," for God. After that, many short, pithy sayings and a few longer discourses urge that we learn from the wisdom and the mistakes of others. God says we do not all have to touch the stove to know it is hot.

The writer of Hebrews admonished, "Remember your leaders, who spoke the word of God to you. Consider the outcome of their way of life and imitate their faith" (Hebrews 13:7). And David, knowing the value of humility, wrote "… a broken and contrite heart, O God, You will not despise" (Psalm 51:17). Both of these verses encourage us as Christians to take direction from other people as well as from God. We are not to be self-contained, unassailable bastions of wisdom and truth. But rather, teachable stones, willing to let God fit us into His spiritual building according to His design and according to what will bring us real satisfaction once the building is up.

Oh, and the hard thing for those who see themselves as God-ordained Correctors of Everyone Else is this: to learn the wisdom of biting the tongue so as to say nothing, though something desperately wants to come out.

THE CONNECTOR

When I became a home owner fourteen years ago, I discovered that I enjoy working with electricity. I'm not an expert in it. I do just simple things, like changing out switches and outlets and adding ground wires. But these simple things bring the house up to code and make it safer, and give a sense of accomplishment. I'm careful to turn circuit breakers off before I do any work so I haven't run excessive numbers of volts through my body. I guess I'm not that much of a thrill-seeker.

At Christmastime we hang icicle lights over the front porch. And we spiral lights around the tree in the living room. Pulling frozen cords apart on the porch, and sliding on my belly under the tree to get to an outlet, used to be required holiday rituals. But I have discovered a better way. There is a neat little device, an electrical connector with a switch on it. You plug your lights into it. Then you plug it into the extension cord. And the switch is conveniently in between. Now I only need to be out on the porch for two seconds when the temperature is twenty below. Now, standing up, I can reach into the center of the tree where I have located the connector. Flick, the lights are on. Click, they're off.

Jesus makes a similar connection between heaven and earth. Paul writes to Timothy, "For there is one God and one mediator between God and men, the man Christ Jesus, who gave Himself as a ransom for all men" (1 Timothy 2:5). And the writer of Hebrews reminds us "... Christ is the mediator of a new covenant, that those who are called may receive the promised eternal inheritance — now that He has died as a ransom to set them free from the sins committed under the first covenant" (Hebrews 9:5). A mediator is one who comes between, a connector of two different things. Jesus connects us sinful people to a holy God when we seek Him by faith. When the connection is made, salvation flows like electricity from heaven to earth. Our human hearts are illuminated with holy light. And darkness, as John writes in his gospel, cannot ever overcome this light again (John 1:5).

Jesus is the only connector that works between God and mankind. He works because He is both God and a man, and connects perfectly between God and men. He works because He is sinless and can be a conduit for God's holiness. He works because He gave His life willingly, out of love for all people, to show the Father's love for all people. Love is why God wanted to make the connection in the first place. Jesus works because He rose again from the dead. Once made, the connection remains unbroken because of His continuing life.

Electrical devices make my life easier, but I could live without them. Jesus, however, is absolutely necessary. To miss that Connector is to remain in spiritual darkness. It is to live without spiritual power. It is to miss life as it was intended by God and it is to miss eternal life. God has already made the connection. But He lets us flip the switch of faith.

THE COST OF LIVING

Rick Carter owns and operates Lucky's Sales and Service. He specializes in trucks and one caught my eye years ago. It was a red Ford F-150 with a six-cylinder engine and two-wheel drive, fairly uncommon in the Northland where most truck owners want off-road capability and a larger engine for towing. I thought about it for a while, went on-line and checked out blue book values and stopped in to make an offer. Rick looked in his file to see what he had into the truck and decided the deal would work. "Take it for a drive," he said. "You'll know soon enough if you want it."

I took it to my usual mechanic to see what he thought about it. The ball joints were good, brakes and tranny seemed all right and it steered true. We were listening to a whistling noise when suddenly the tension pulley near the alternator froze and the engine shut off. "I guess that was the whistling noise," I said. I have a keen grasp of the obvious. Rick came with a wrecker and towed it back to his shop.

His crew replaced the tension pulley. The "check engine" light stayed on however. After putting the truck on a scanner Rick found a problem with the flaps in the intake manifold. They were sticking and causing the engine to run too lean. His guys unstuck the flaps and put in a new gasket. The truck ran fine for a while and then the "check engine" light came on again. Pretty soon there were new plugs and wires and an oxygen sensor. The "check engine" light stayed off and I began a final evaluation.

When I buy a vehicle, I push every button, turn every knob, run the wipers and fan, try all the door locks. And in the case of a truck, try to lower the tailgate. It stuck. Fortunately one of Rick's mechanics knew the magic place to push to get it to open. Rick had the tailgate panel removed and the gate mechanism lubricated. Everything was fixed and working. The price of the truck stayed the same. So I bought it.

Sometimes the margin of profit on a vehicle is not too large, and the vehicle begins to cost more than can be recovered in a sale. None of the things that went wrong were wrong when Rick acquired the truck. To his credit, he stayed with my offer and maintained the integrity of selling only when the vehicle was in good running order.

When a person decides to turn his or her life over to Jesus, there is a cost. No one knows ahead of time what the cost will be. There is usually a sense that it will be steep but also that it will be worth it. So people start in. Sometimes the cost comes in terms of friends, as healthy patterns replace unhealthy ones and the old friends find the person "too religious." Sometimes finances suffer as the pursuit of money isn't as satisfying as it once was. All kinds of "personal advantages" disappear when it no longer seems right to cheat or to steal or to bend the truth or to be selfish. And some folks give up when they see it isn't to their "profit" to be a Christian.

Jesus asked those who wished to follow Him to consider carefully whether or not they would be able to stick with their commitment. Exaggerating to make His point, He once said, "If anyone comes to me and does not hate his father and mother, his wife and children, his brothers and sisters—yes, even his own life—he cannot be my disciple" (Luke 14:26).

To be a follower of Jesus requires more than some are willing to give. There is a cost. We shouldn't hide that fact. But in the end, a life lived for Jesus is the only life worth living. I don't know if that can be understood apart from actually trying it and experiencing it to be true. The chief reason for trying it is what Jesus has into the deal: His own life, expended on the cross for our mistakes and "breakdowns".

And His resurrection from the dead is the warranty we get, promising our own eternal life, and promising that the cost of our living for Him is worth it.

THE HIKE

For over a year I preached through the Gospel of Mark because I wanted to get to know Jesus better. That sounds so good, but really it was because He is somewhat of a mystery to me.

My life of faith is like a hike. I have been on the hike now for over forty years. And I am still trying to get a handle on the Leader. Sometimes He takes us to an absolutely breathtaking overlook. Sometimes He traverses difficult ground. For me it is mostly walking and climbing. Which is fine, but I guess I expected something different. Maybe a chance to hang-glide off a majestic summit at some point.

In the Gospel I keep reading about His teaching that drew people like a magnet, authority that surpassed human powers of persuasion, signs and wonders that confirmed the words He spoke. Though I am certain He has this kind of power, I have not seen too much of it in my life or ministry. I have not seen a short leg grow longer or a person rise from the dead or salmon multiplied at a potluck where the food ran short, as some of my Pentecostal friends have. And I have not been swallowed up in the love of God like some desert father monks I have read about. Christian "survivalists," and people obsessed with eschatology, and prophet chasers, and square-cornered guardians of truth and certain Christian musicians seem to know Him much better than I do. Minor miracles, modest love and some disappointments have been my lot. Not that I am dissatisfied. Well, maybe a little.

At times the hike has seemed like a lonely path, like the starless trail I walked down on the way to my deer stand one pre-dawn November morning. That day I wondered if hell might be an even lonelier trail, from which you can hear the sounds of humanity off in the distance, like trucks on the highway and railroad trains rolling through the countryside, but from which you can never get to any other human being.

I have enthusiastically invited others to join the hike and follow Jesus, and some have. For which I am grateful, to the point of being overwhelmed each time it happens. I know that Jesus is amazing. I believe everything written about Him and said by Him. I know Him personally and yet not well enough. Not the way I want to anyway. I keep trying to understand this Friend Who is God, who deals with each person a little differently. I signed up for the duration, and I mean to finish the hike well. But sometimes I feel like I am on a slightly different trail than everyone else. Could that be by His arrangement?

THE HITCHHIKER

He was standing on the sidewalk in front of the Pro Fuel station, the collar of his black jacket turned up against the wind and a black stocking cap pulled down to cover his ears. Dark eyes darted behind silver-rimmed glasses. His long hair seemed to be trying to escape from under the cap. A short, dark beard obscured his face. In his gloved hands he held a small cardboard sign reading "Grand Rapids."

I had no intention of taking him there. I had no intention of even picking him up. But I judged that he wasn't any taller than I am, and that reduced the risk in my mind. When I pulled over, he hurried away from my truck, which confused me, until I realized he was retrieving a very large suitcase on wheels. We hoisted it into the bed of the truck and headed slowly up Highway 2.

There is an exhortation in the New Testament which says, "Do not neglect to show hospitality to strangers, for by this some have entertained angels without knowing it" (Hebrews 13:2). Hitchhikers, as a general population, don't support beatific expectations. Still, I was drawn to him, and a voice I have come to trust as belonging to the Holy Spirit let me know it was safe. We did end up going all the way to Grand Rapids,

Minnesota. His story was compelling, and it took that long to hear it.

He had been a Druid—part of a group which in ancient times launched the day we call Halloween. He had been a Pagan—a person opposed to Christianity, and also a white supremacist. He had been a drug user. And he had served eleven years in prison for a crime he did not divulge. Having lost his license to drive, he was hitchhiking to see his children, who had become young adults.

What was most compelling was the part of the story in which his life was transformed. In prison he found freedom. Some Christians came in and began to tell about Jesus and how He changes people on the inside. At first he didn't want anything to do with Jesus. But their love for him was genuine, and he knew he needed and wanted that. So he gave up his rights to himself, his associations with the groups he had known, the friends who really weren't friends, and he began a vastly different life. He found help in the Bible, prayer, a mentor and a good church in Minneapolis. And he got a valued job in the warehouse of a publishing company.

He had a lot of questions, like how do predestination and free will operate in the same universe? We did not solve that completely. More importantly, he wanted to know how to forgive his father for mistreating him while growing up. We did not solve that completely either. But when he reflected on his own metamorphosis, and on being a different kind of father to his children, he had hope that someday he and his father would both be ready to reconcile.

Even though my life's work is all about faith, there are days when I wonder what I believe and why. Discouragement makes a person doubt even firm convictions. Things spin out of control. Disappointment comes. Relationships go south. Bad decisions are made. Work is ineffective. Each hour robs more joy. Then a miracle happens.

There are many kinds of miracles, but the ones most convincing to me are the ongoing ones in which a life is radically improved by the Radical Improver. Like the life of a hitchhiker, for example. I got to see it firsthand. This stranger embodied the reassurance I needed. He became a friend and brother in the Lord.

And for one more day, I too believed.

THE INADEQUACY OF MATHEMATICS

In his book *Cries of the Heart*, Ravi Zacharias deals with the matter of loneliness, which is common to humanity. We all seek to be in satisfying relationships, but in the absence of such relationships, we will turn to other things to "fill the hole." We want to get along with others in our world, but are not always sure how to do it. What we are trying to do, he says, is "fill the *whole* of our lives" with love.

F.W. Boreham connects the love we need to personhood. He writes about Solomon's dilemma with the two prostitutes of 1 Kings 3:16-28. They both gave birth about the same time, and one of the prostitutes rolled over on her child in the night and smothered it. So she took the other woman's child and claimed it was her own. The case came before the king and he decided to cut the remaining living child in two, a fair mathematical answer to the problem. But half a child plus half a child do not add up to a whole person. The true mother pleaded to keep the child intact, even if she herself could not raise it. By this affirmation of personhood, Solomon knew who the true mother was, and where the true love was. He gave her the living child.

People are not mathematical quantities, says F.W. Boreham, they are personal entities. Only a whole person can love and be loved. God in Christ, the Divine Whole Person, has loved us first and best. And when we put our trust in Him, we find we can love too. We start by loving God. Other relationships follow. All of these relationships, with God and with others, address our loneliness. Mathematics, which deals with half-persons, is inadequate to meet our need for companionship and personal love. But God, Who is love personified, can well fill our "whole."

THE INSCRUTABLE INSTRUMENT PANEL

~~~

We own a 1998 Dodge Caravan. It's the short one, with some features like power windows, mirrors and door locks, but no CD player, compass or outdoor thermometer. We bought it with 48,000 miles and the odometer now reads 148,000 miles. The seats are comfortable, the rust so far manageable. For the most part it is a trustworthy vehicle. But it does have this one quality, shared by others of its kind, which we find a bit unnerving: every so often the instrument panel blanks out.

    Driving along and glancing down at the panel we can see the engine temperature is fine, the alternator is charging the battery, we are within the speed limit and we are in the proper gear. Then suddenly, Poof! And we don't know how fast we are going, how much gas is left in the tank or what the rpms are. The check engine light comes on and the ABS light comes on. Headlights keep working, the low fuel warning bell still functions, nobody's seat ejects, but it's a bit strange, especially at night when there is supposed to be a comforting glow of gauges in soft green light and we have a blackout. So far the instrument panel has always returned after an interval. The power locks suddenly click down and the gauges light up and we breathe a sigh of relief. We've spent considerable time diagnosing the problem and finding ways to shorten the interval, to better control the electrical system. We have learned that sometimes we get gauges back if we disconnect the battery briefly and hook it up again, or if we replace the instrument panel. Or the chassis brain box.

We have not replaced the chassis brain box because new ones cost six hundred dollars and you cannot find a used one with exactly the right code and features to match the one you have. And if you could, you would have to stand on your head and wedge your face behind the brake pedal and loosen the un-findable screw that holds the box in, and then change the box out. I know all this because I have removed the unit in anticipation of replacing it, only to discover that used ones are not available. A friend who works on these kinds of vehicles said, "Buy some quick-drying electrical cleaner and spray it on the connections that go to the instrument panel and the chassis brain box." We did, and it worked, and so we have done that from time to time. It is a ten dollar fix. Of course this last time, it didn't work. So we are waiting for the gauges to come back when they decide it is time. All we know for sure is that the instrument panel is inscrutable. We've done our best to "scrute," but we may never understand it. The van runs just fine and we live with some mystery.

It is not so different with God, albeit there is nothing wrong with Him. Simply put, He is inscrutable. He is a unique Being, with thoughts and ways far beyond our own. He seems to disappear and then reappear. He works in patterns we can identify and then He doesn't. He communicates clearly and then He is silent. He answers prayer right away and then He keeps us waiting for a long stretch. Over time the question becomes: "Will we trust Him when we do not know what He is doing, when He does not act according to our expectations?" The essence of faith is just that. Trusting when there is mystery about God.

We do know some things beyond a shadow of a doubt. We know that He loves us because He sent His Son, Jesus, to reveal His character and die the death we deserved for our sins. We know that Jesus rose from the dead after three days, demonstrating His power over sin and death. We know that He gives joy and peace when joy and peace should not be ours because of circumstances. We know that He continues to do many miracles.

Faith in God is well placed ... but you may not want to buy my van.

THE MOST TRUSTED MAN

Walter Cronkite passed away at the age of ninety-two. Tom Brokaw's National View article said that Cronkite was a man of many sides: sailor, race-car driver, bon vivant (a French phrase meaning "good companion"), journalist and role model to those who shared his profession. He was in the middle of the biggest stories of his time for half a century. Perhaps the greatest tribute, however, was naming him "the most trusted man in America," an honor bestowed upon him by his own countrymen.

As I reflect on my own life and the reputation of the Church in America, I wonder if we enjoy such favor with our countrymen. I remember a poll taken when I was newer to the ministry which rated ministers below pharmacists in trustworthiness. It stung. Nor do churches always have a good reputation. Congregations sometimes misbehave or become ingrown or argue more than they are at peace, and the Gospel gets a black eye.

Positions of great visibility carry a coincident responsibility. Jesus always handled His visibility well. And He handled responsibility well. He was "the most trusted man" in all of history. Why? Because He spoke the truth. He kept His word. He did not go back on any promises. He treated people with respect and kindness, and extended this even to His enemies. He did not hold grudges, nor did He seek revenge. He was not self-absorbed or self-serving, but genuinely sought the best for others, without exhibiting partiality or prejudice. He sacrificed Himself for the world.

THE OLD LANTERN

It was a treasure unearthed during one of Eric's many summer garage sale excursions. Eric is my friend and he is a marvel to watch. He hops out of his van and is halfway up the driveway before the wheels stop rolling. He is amiable and affable, and has an eye for value. He often locates things for others. He seeks out railroad artifacts for me, which is how I got the lantern.

The aluminum case was pretty rusty when I got it onto my workbench. Unlike most of the lanterns Eric has found which burn kerosene, this one was electric. Its bulb was housed under a little wire cage, and the pear-shaped globe was so fused to the battery compartment that I could not separate one from the other.

It was manufactured by the Embury Company of Warsaw, New York and it was old. The instructions on the red paper in the battery compartment say to face the brass caps of the battery "cells" toward the hinge of the compartment. Brass-capped batteries are no longer made. I cleaned it up a bit, but I doubted it would ever work. Still, I got to wondering … As I sanded with emery cloth and fiddled with the slide switch, a thought developed in my mind about how the lantern was like a human life—some parts not together, while others are fused so tightly they do not move. The corrosion inside was a good metaphor for sin, and the lack of batteries explained a lack of God's Spirit. Ezekiel 37 came to mind, the vision of the valley of dry bones. In the passage the bones represent the people of Israel in exile, hoping to be reconnected with kindred and homeland and to be given new life. God asked Ezekiel if he thought the bones could live. Ezekiel wasn't sure. God showed him in the vision that they could live. And then God made history follow the vision. The people returned from exile in Babylon and the nation was reconstituted. I also thought of 2 Corinthians 5:17: "If anyone is in Christ, that person is a new creation ..." Pretty soon I was on a mission and had to know if the lantern could live again.

I bought D size cells, and found that some are just slightly larger than others. Only the smaller ones fit properly. The spring brass connectors were pretty far gone and I damaged one further using a Dremel tool while sanding it, so had to make a new one. I took the lantern to North Place, my oldest son's residential group home, on the night I led Bible Study. I made a presentation about how a ruined life can be redeemed. Whether the lantern would work was uncertain. It had been intermittent all day. I prayed it would "live," and when I slid the switch over, the light came on. It was a small miracle!

The whole world was in need of a miracle when Caesar Augustus was Emperor in Rome, Quirinius was Governor of Syria and Herod was King in Judea. And then God slid over the switch of history and the Light of the world came on. That was the first Christmas. I don't know what kinds of things are rusty, ugly, stuck, corroded, damaged or empty in your life, but I know that God can give newness and much needed light, through Jesus, on a day when it just has to be there.

His work is miraculous and eternal, and if you need to "live," it is His workbench you want to be on. He can make it happen.

The lantern is in my office now. I keep it as a symbol of hope and a reminder of the power God has to resurrect dead things. Like me. Like you.

THE PARABLE OF THE RIGHTEOUS AND REBELLIOUS MACHINES

(The writing style of this parable was inspired by "Parables of a Country Parson," by William E. Barton.)

And it came to pass on a certain day, that I journeyed forth into mine estate, that I might complete my yard work before the Sabbath. For lo, the grass did grow long and prosper and threatened to swallow my children in their play; and the garden didst flourish in its effort, but only in regard to weeds. So I journeyed forth as far as the back garage, where my heart was gladdened by the sight of two machines. And the one machine was a lawnmower, and the other was a tiller of the soil.

And behold, the lawnmower was a righteous machine, for having been filled with oil and gas, yea even 30W oil and premium gas, did it start easily, though it was new and not used to starting. In truth, only six times did I prime the carburetor before the mower didst roar to life and run strong. In straight paths did it walk before me, swerving neither to the right nor to the left. And my children didst rejoice to see an emerald carpet appearing, and they were exceedingly glad. Except my younger son, whose sister caused him to examine closely a dandelion plant, to which he was allergic. And the mower was simple in operation and steady in performance, and in not much time at all did it render the grass to be of the proper height.

And it came to pass that, encouraged by the righteous mower, I prayed the LORD to expand my success in labor, though not mine actual territory, lest it become too much for me and I die before my time.

And I beheld in the back garage the tiller. Now the tiller was not a new machine, but not therefore to be despised. For I didst reason within myself that it had a glorious history and record of service and much charm, though the name of the manufacturer was long ago rubbed off. But it was a rebellious machine and contrary. For though I didst entreat it with oil and gas and much fine gear grease, as much as it would hold so that the abundance ran down upon my beard and onto the floor, not would it start. All day long didst I seek to start it. Nor did I yank upon the cord in wrath. Moreover didst I remove the air cleaner cover and comprehend the choke mechanism and fiddle with each of the four set screws, none of which seemed to have any bearing on the operation of the tiller, leastwise not the starting thereof.

And behold, I didst lift up mine eyes to the street, where I had several things set out for sale. And as I contemplated having the tiller join them, didst it have a change of heart and repent of its folly and consent to start, though it spat gas in my face and caused me to breathe noxious fumes and burned my hand on its muffler. Yet finally didst it perform its function, and till the soil of the garden, and dig up many wondrous bugs and worms. And so it returned to its place in the garage as the spring rains began gently to fall.

And I meditated on the events of the day, and perceived that there are people in the world like these two machines. For there are those who start well and run smoothly and seek to please God and to use their strength to establish His purposes on earth. Likewise are there those who do not start well, do nothing smoothly and are a vexation to their Owner, who burn God's hand and are in peril of winding up at the street with the things for sale. They only grudgingly fulfill their purpose and are only vaguely aware that they belong to the God Who sustains them.

Yet doth God love these two kinds of people with an equal love. With one kind He is pleased; and with the other He is patient. And His word doth declare that there is more joy in heaven over one rebellious person who repents than over ninety-nine righteous people who need not repent (Luke 15:7). And a great miracle of life doth occur, perhaps the greatest of all miracles, when a change of heart is wrought in the rebellious person by God's persistent love and mercy.

THE PARABLE OF THE SPARK PLUG

There once was a spark plug, which thought it was something out of the ordinary. It imagined itself to be the key operation in a glorious machine, but in reality was just a part in a gas lawnmower, and an old mower at that. The paint on the mower was faded. The wheels were slanted with respect to the deck. The pull cord was frayed. The mower idled unevenly and seemed ready to stall with each crescendo and diminuendo of the tired engine. But whenever someone primed the carburetor and yanked the cord, the plug fired off with pride.

The plug was a study in hubris. It was proud of its AC Delco heritage. It was proud of the numbers stamped on its ceramic insulator. It was proud of the threads along the reach that held it tightly in the cylinder. It was even proud of the carbon accumulating on the electrodes. It considered itself mature, hard-working and worldly wise, and it fairly exploded with self-importance.

Then one day something odd happened. Or rather, it didn't happen. Someone primed the carburetor and yanked on the cord. Gas spurted into the cylinder. The

Backward Glances: Faith Through a Rearview Mirror

plug readied itself for the usual start up. But nothing happened. Nothing at all. There was more priming, more gas spurting, more yanking and still nothing. Someone else came over to look at the mower. After some consultation there was more yanking. Then a little pause and renewed yanking. The first someone yanked. The second someone yanked. Nothing. The spark plug was puzzled. It didn't know what was wrong, but it was quite certain that it was not the problem.

A third someone came over from next door. More yanking. Then a pause for reflection. The third someone asked permission to take the mower to a garage where there were some tools. The spark plug was miffed. The mower had worked fine just a week ago. Some part was just not doing its job.

At the garage, the third someone checked the oil and put a little in. And the gas, and put a little in. But that didn't fix anything really. Then there was the strangest sensation for the plug as it felt itself fitted with a socket and rotated counterclockwise. The plug was slipped out of the cylinder. It felt exposed. The third someone examined the plug closely and muttered something not entirely complimentary. The plug was insulted, indignant. It was a plug of pedigree and had been offended. The electrodes were brushed roughly with a brass brush and sanded clean with emery cloth. Disoriented and angry, the plug was fitted back into the socket and screwed back into the cylinder.

The carburetor was primed. The gas spurted. The cord was yanked. The plug fired. The mower was alive again. Shocked and surprised, the plug reviewed the events of the last few moments. There was only one conclusion to be drawn. It had been the problem after all. Its pedigree had not helped. Its pride had not helped. The skilled hands of someone bigger than the plug, bigger than the engine, bigger than the mower had worked a work of grace. And had given the plug its place and its purpose. The plug's anger dissolved. Its arrogance slipped away.

And with each detonation, it spoke its gratitude to one who knew it better than it knew itself.

THE PILE OF STUFF

It started with a note from our office administrator. The trustees, who oversee the church building, were about to clear the landing midway between the sanctuary and a temporary upstairs office. The office had been used during a building project and a fair amount of my stuff ended up on that landing. If I wanted control over it, I had to act before they got to it. The trustees are super people. But how would they know what value to assign to the things they found? So on a Tuesday morning I carried the stuff from the landing to my new office thinking, "It shouldn't be too hard to go through."

The pile didn't reach to the ceiling, but it swallowed a sizeable area of carpet. A dozen years' accumulation makes its presence felt. There were past bulletins, sermon notes, maps of the Holy Land, Confirmation books, staples, some pictures I had decided not to hang, and the odd pen with our church name misspelled. All this I had expected.

I had forgotten about the collected bits of personal history. Like the log cabin church, made out of dowel rods by a fellow I knew who had spent time in jail. It was a gift for keeping in touch with him during a wasted stretch of his life. And the baseball from a man whose funeral I had done, who lived like a hermit in Superior,

Wisconsin. His apartment had been drowned with papers and notes about movies and train schedules and the local minor league baseball games. The notes had meaning only for him. There was the poster-size picture of Jesus' nail-scarred hands, drawn and colored by one of our teens. The hands reach out to receive you, or to hold you up if you turn the picture upside down. And the black boom box with two cassette tape decks, outdated now. It played the music of Christian artists while puppets lip-synched harmoniously in the window of a homemade theater. What was I to do with those things?

I didn't want to lose the memories. Even the painful ones. I have a rock that is red as if stained with blood, a memento of a funeral done for a young college student and rock climber, who committed suicide on Park Point in Duluth, Minnesota. And a statue of Jesus knocking on a door, hoping to come in. It was given to me by a woman who left the church when we could not be happy that she moved in with a man who abandoned his wife, after the wife developed Parkinson's disease. And old directories, listing families that no longer come to our fellowship for reasons I have not always understood and they could not always explain. And the Instant Miracle Shoe Shine, which was given to me by a colleague in ministry, vital into his eighties. He knew Billy Graham personally and would have gone to one of Billy's birthday celebrations, but cancer interrupted his plans. His life fell under the control of family members in another state, who did not know who he was in this state. These are not my favorite recollections. They illustrate what the theologian and author William Willimon once said: "Ministry is messy." Still the recollections are important.

Often in Scripture, God's people are asked to remember something important. For example, Jesus, at the Last Supper, asked His closest friends to remember *Him* as often as they would eat bread and drink a cup. Communion has become our most significant way of connecting with Him and His death on the cross. What He did on the cross was unexpected, unforgettable, unparalleled and messy. It also gives us hope, because Someone loved us enough to die in our place for our sins.

I did not keep everything in my pile of stuff. I did not need to. But I did keep the things that help me to remember Jesus, His love and His sacrifice. The rest had to go and tossing out took considerable time. Drat those office administrators and their notes.

THE RIGHT STUFF INSIDE

Sheldon, Missouri looks like a ghost town. It is not quite that deserted, but nearly so. Most of the stores along Main Street are closed. Many do not even have old signs indicating what businesses used to be there. A block from the water tower, however, is a thriving enterprise—the Jones Boot Company. A big sign on US Highway 71 advertizes 6,000 pairs of boots. The Internet site says there are over 400 styles, and hats, belts and jewelry as well. The store is sided with faded gray barn wood, a western façade rising from the low-roofed porch. And there is a big red plastic boot attached to the façade over the front door. I am a boot wearer and so, on our way back from visiting family in Arkansas one summer, we had to stop.

Gold being pretty valuable, I had sold my high school class ring, hoping to get enough for a pair of stingray boots. I was after stingray because the leather is almost indestructible. You can take a pocket knife and scrape on the toe of the boot and not scratch it. The Jones Boot Company had stingray boots in my size. And because the company gives discounts to police officers, fire fighters and clergy, I could afford them. I came home with a great looking pair of stingray boots, dyed black, with a diamond of natural, off-white color on each instep.

What is significant about the Jones Boot Company is its ability to do well, even in a town that is not doing well, and in an economy that is uncertain and sometimes hard on small businesses. The company has expanded twice since 1973 and has increased from two to nine employees. It was busy the day we stopped. The company credits exceptional service, fine products and attractive prices for its success. It has the right stuff inside its walls.

There is a spiritual parallel. Surrounded by disheartening circumstances, little encouragement, perhaps even hostile influences, a person may thrive. Having the right stuff inside is what makes a difference.

A former Director of World Missions for our denomination was visiting Burkina Faso, one of the poorest nations in Africa and in the world. He met a woman there who was elderly and dying of cancer. Her daughter and grandchild both had contracted AIDS. He felt overwhelmed by all that she was experiencing and wondered what comfort might be given to her, what words might soothe some of the intense suffering. "How are you doing?" he asked. To his great surprise she responded, "I'm doing fine. I know Jesus."

The Jones Boot Company and the woman in Burkina Faso both figured it out. Anyone can thrive with the right stuff inside.

THE SOUR NEED

One Sunday night in April I found myself speeding north in the passenger seat of a tan Buick with my friend, a retired plumber. We were heading for Zim, a sprawling metropolis the width of an eye blink on Highway 27 in northern Minnesota. Zim is situated in lowlands which seem likely to sink into the earth if the atmospheric pressure becomes too great.

There is a little white church there—Evangelical Free, if it matters—neither proud nor imposing, a too-steep wooden ramp approaching the door from one side, and plain wooden steps approaching from the front. The ramp ices over at a certain temperature and seems to have been built more for the entertainment of those who don't need it than for ingress. Just inside the door, the tiny narthex opens left and there is a shelf for a coffee pot, a jug of juice and two large boxes of day old pastries. Opposite is a stairway to the basement and the restroom. The restroom has plumbing supplies handy: floats, pipes, handles and such, as if they might be needed directly.

The evening service is mainly a gospel sing, led by a fellow with a banjo and a flair for dramatic reading and humor. Several guitars and a tambourine also grace the platform. The accordion was missing the night I went, but we made do. Flannel and jeans are the uniform, except for the dog which, having been recently clipped, came in a pink satin shirt.

People don't stand on formality. They sing and fellowship and get refreshments and listen to God's Word and maybe some other inspirational thoughts from a Christian author, but at that service there is no preaching. Different musicians take turns leading, the dog drinks juice out of everyone's Styrofoam cup, announcements about community pancake feeds are made, cards are signed for servicemen and servicewomen on active duty, and everybody prays.

It was the prayer that caught my attention that night. One particular request was made on behalf of a person suffering with cancer. At the end of it, the petitioner asked for God's help in "the sour need."

Well it wasn't that of course. I had heard it wrong. It was a prayer for God's help in "this hour of need." But as I thought about it, I realized that my different interpretation wasn't a bad one. Cancer is sour, as are so many things in this life: Parkinson's Disease, ALS, suicide, school shootings, child abuse, autoimmune disorders, brain damage, divorce, accidental drowning, bankruptcy, job loss ...

Into infirmities and circumstances such as these comes our God. Some think Him to be the cruel perpetrator of what goes wrong. Others think not, but are angry with Him for not preventing tragedy. My experience is that He is the One who enters the sour moments and finds a way to turn them to good. Not to something sweet, but to something good, using whatever faith He finds among the people involved.

The people in Zim are real people, faith-filled people, living with real challenges. There isn't much need for, or attempt at, pretense. They speak the truth about themselves and about the world they live in. And they know a real God, Who helps them in their "sour need."

THE TOTAL LOSS DEPARTMENT

❦

When you call my auto insurance company and punch in extension fifty-three, a cheerful representative answers, gives her name and tells you that you have reached the Total Loss Department. That is what they call it right up front. And you know then, if not before, that the accident you were in has resulted in damages that exceed the worth of your car. At least as far as the insurance company is concerned.

I was in one of those accidents in June, 2010 on the way to the Evangelical Covenant Church's Annual Meeting in Minneapolis. I had taken Highway 61 south through the countryside, hoping to stop in Cambridge and see some relatives before continuing to the Twin Cities. But about four miles outside Mora, on the stretch that joins Highway 23, where there is a huge, green arrow stuck into the ground in someone's yard, as if shot from heaven, I had a meeting with a large doe.

Rain poured down as the doe skipped across the pavement. She leaped into the air. I stood on the brakes. We tried to miss each other but we both failed. She crashed onto my windshield, kicking a wrinkle into the driver's side fender on the way. I stayed put, stunned and wondering if an airbag was going to deploy. It didn't. The Good Samaritan who stopped to help me said the doe bounced fifteen feet above the car before landing in the grass at the side of the road. Happily, both the doe and I walked away from the encounter. A week later I returned to Don's Auto in Ogilvie where the car had been towed, to get my "personal effects." More evidence that something had "died" and was totally lost. Actually the car wasn't totally lost. Only the windshield and fender were damaged. It was very repairable. And I was sorely tempted to have it fixed because it was a convertible. And because, as is the case with many of us, a lot of my identity was wrapped up in that car. But instead of fixing it, I let it go. Here is why.

When you get things fixed, it is like hitting an "undo" button on the computer. You erase the mistake, the accident, and maybe pull out some dents in your own identity. While it is wonderful to get things fixed, in this case it was better for me to let it go and remember that my identity is in Christ. The in-CAR-nation that really matters in the grand scheme, the embodiment of any good character I may possess, has to do with Jesus, not the big iron thing I drive. And while the convertible was a great road machine, my wife and kids were never too fond of it. The vinyl top had a big blind spot where the rear window would be in a sedan, and that made the other drivers in our home a little anxious. I did not want to have a blind spot where possessions were concerned. I wanted people to know they were more important than a car. I wanted my priorities to be right. So, the two kids who were still at home, and who were just starting to drive, got to help pick out the replacement. I wanted them to know they were valued by giving them a voice in the matter. Home life is better if it doesn't have to be dad's way all the time.

The "total loss" went to the auto auction in St. Paul. Hopefully, someone with skill and money bought it and restored it. We moved on to the next iron thing. It was not new. And it did not cost much because we did not get much for the wrecked one. Dodge Shadows aren't so valuable that you get a big settlement when they're wrecked. But the "new" car was just fine because it got us where we needed to go. It was a Chevy Cavalier and got thirty miles per gallon. The convertible did not have pre-eminence over any people, which was as it should be. The new car didn't either. The "total loss" resulted in some important gains for me and for my family. And, truth be told, I kind of liked the new one. But don't tell anybody.

THE VALUE OF FAIRY TALES

I have been reading G.K. Chesterton's autobiography entitled *Orthodoxy*, in which he explained how he became a Christian. Chesterton really had no intention of becoming a Christian. In fact he was out to create his own new heresy. But when he got it all put together, he discovered that it had already been done, and that it was in fact orthodox Christianity. It surprised him as much as anyone.

By "orthodox" Chesterton meant those beliefs common to Christians around the world, as set forth in The Apostles' Creed. He was one of the great thinkers Christianity has had, and one of its great apologists, helping others to see what Christianity is all about and why it makes sense.

Anticipating a reasoned apologetic from him, I was taken aback when I read, "My first and last philosophy, that which I believe in with unbroken certainty, I learnt in the nursery." What he referred to was fairy tales. Though unexpected (much of his writing is unexpected), it actually makes sense. At our earliest age, we learn stories, seemingly impossible and untrue, which nevertheless convey strong Biblical truth.

For example, "Jack the Giant Killer" explains that some giants should be killed, especially the one named

Pride. "Cinderella" teaches the same lesson as Mary's *Magnificat* (the song of praise to God after Mary finds out she will bear the Christ Child): namely that God exalts the humble. "Beauty and the Beast" tells that a thing must be loved before it is loveable, and God has made us loveable by loving us. "Sleeping Beauty" is perhaps the best example, reminding us that "the human creature was blessed with all birthday gifts, yet cursed with death; and how death also may perhaps be softened to a sleep." By God's design the writers of fairy tales may have set down more than they realized, more about reality than we usually suspect. God delights in hiding truth in all kinds of places, hoping that we will find it.

THEY KNOW ...

The fourth Tuesday of the month is my night to go to my son's residential group home in Duluth, Minnesota and lead Bible study. I really enjoy it. Two group homes owned by the Covenant combine for dinner and Bible study. The food is always great, and the guys are excited about everything—what's for dinner, how their favorite sports teams are doing or what funny thing one of the staff said.

One of my turns fell on January 22, 2005. Several guys were anticipating playing in the worship band. We have an electric guitar, two acoustic guitars, a violin, a harmonica, a cowbell and sometimes a keyboard. The Patriots and Giants were less than two weeks away from facing off in the Super Bowl (the Patriots won). And that night was also the anniversary of Roe vs. Wade, the landmark court decision which made abortion a matter of legal choice.

Having participated in the Jericho March downtown at noon, the sanctity of life was on my mind. The march is named after the famous march of the Israelis around the walls of Jericho, which fell down when the people raised a great shout. It is the hope of the current march organizers that the law allowing abortion on demand will someday fall down.

I took a photo of a child with me to Bible Study and showed it around. Everyone there knew that the child was not yet born. Two of the guys knew the child was in the early stages of development. One was within a week of knowing exactly how old the child was—sixteen weeks. One of the guys knew of a passage in Psalm 139 which speaks of God forming children in the womb and numbering their days before they are born. We talked about the Christmas story, and how Jesus had looked just like the child in the picture at one point. We also read a passage from Genesis, in which God is thinking out loud about making mankind in His own image. I asked what the similarity might be between the child in the picture and God. Without any hesitation one of the guys answered, "Both are living souls." That stunned me. Another one of the guys went on to explain how human beings are unique in having souls among all that is created. You might think I led them on to that conclusion. I didn't. I hadn't even thought of it.

Each of the guys in the two group homes has challenges. Represented among them is lower than average IQ, traumatic brain injury, obsessive-compulsive disorder, Asperger's syndrome, schizophrenia, bi-polar disorder, microcephalic disorder, agenesis of the corpus colossum (when the two sides of the brain don't talk to each other) and pervasive developmental disorder. Yet, they are spiritually astute. I think that is because they don't wrestle with things to the extent that a moral issue is contorted into one about politics or civil rights.

We prayed at the end of the study. Some of the guys prayed for family members who had experienced recent loss, or the soldiers serving in the Iraqi conflict, or a peer. Some prayed for the cause of life. It was a way of taking responsibility.

A deacon in a Michigan church I served thought we as Christians ought to go a step further than prayer. He did not have much use for judgmental Christians who define themselves by what they are against. Rather, he said, we ought to love mothers who might be contemplating abortion for whatever reason, and we ought to love the children waiting to be born. And if we are really serious, we ought to consider supporting those mothers and helping to raise those children. The guys at the study thought that was a pretty good idea too. They know right from wrong. And they know the value of life. Some able-bodied folks do not have that kind of understanding. But the guys with developmental challenges know. The Apostle Paul wrote to his friends in Corinth, Greece, "God chose the foolish things of the world to shame the wise" (1 Corinthians 1:27).

TOO CLOSE TO THE WORK

Twenty-some years ago, a friend gave me some Lionel trains to go with one I had purchased (used) for my older son for Christmas. That son Ryan is now grown and on his own and I have inherited all of the trains. There are two steam engines and a diesel engine. The layout is in the basement. It consists of two loops, one inside the other, set up so the trains can pass each other going in opposite directions

I have never had a lot of money to spend on scenery, so most of it is homemade. A water tower started out as a peanut can, a trackside tap was originally a Foster's beer can I found on the road. (Australians put beer in big cans!) Office buildings were fabricated from light bulb cartons turned inside out, rock formations were simulated from buffalo board covered with sheetrock compound, pine forests were made from artificial Christmas trees (actual moss from the northern Minnesota Boundary Waters Canoe Area hanging from them). There is an epoxy stream, a harbor and a fishing boat and several deciduous trees made out of weeds dipped in green paint. A little town with a lighted church and a number of painted people fill up the miniature world. In a visit to Carr's Hobby Shop I purchased an old ZW transformer, a wonderful power source that runs both trains at once, blows the whistles and causes the trains to change directions.

One project leads to another, and soon I was lubricating engines, adding side spurs to the track and wondering how I could make a good thing better. It was then I noticed that the diesel engine has a horn and a light. They had never worked so I hadn't paid much attention. Now I was paying attention, and I set about to make everything do what it is supposed to do.

Under the cover of the diesel engine I found a socket in need of a light bulb, a battery compartment in need of a D-cell to run the horn, and a couple of wires that needed re-soldering. Bending over the work bench, eyes focused on some small detail, I pushed a pinkie finger right into the hot soldering iron. Natural consequences being a good teacher, and I being of an intelligent bent, I only needed to do that once.

It got me to thinking whether I don't sometimes get so wrapped up in details that I miss something important in the broader picture. Take Christmas, for instance. There are so many details to the season—gifts, decorations, meals, concerts, travel plans, stretching the money, special services, keeping feuding relatives apart, sending out cards, avoiding lutefisk. It is easy to lose the broader picture. Which is this: God came to earth as one of us, for our joy and His joy. Simple and sweet. One of His names says it: Immanuel—"God with us."

Our family likes Christmas music. There is a rule in the house that it is not played until *after* Thanksgiving. We try to buy a new CD each year, and one year there was a song that made me pause. Wrapped up in the details of a hard life, the lyricist wrote about missing the coming of the world's Savior. With obvious regret the words poured out: "Forgive us, Lord. We didn't know it was You."

It is easy to get too close to the Christmas "work." But I do not have to. I can keep the big picture in view. We ministers are supposed to do that, but we're not any better at it than anyone else. I pray for eyes to see the most important thing rather than the most pressing thing. I pray for eyes to see Him.

TRACTION

~~~~

Some well deserved ribbing comes my way because I change cars rather frequently. I figure there are a fair number of really good ones out there, different kinds, and I am trying to own one of each while there is time.

The current car is an '03 Chevy Cavalier. Before that was a '93 Dodge Shadow convertible. Before that a '97 Suburau Legacy Outback wagon. Before that a '97 Ford F-150 pick-up. Before that a pimped out '01 PT Cruiser (it was metallic blue with aqua flames). Before that ... there were others.

The '97 Subaru Legacy Outback Wagon was not terribly impressive. And I did not pay a lot for it. But I put a lot of money into it. Almost everything that breaks or wears out on a Subaru is expensive to fix. Even the things that do not end in "-or" like the radiator and the alternator. I never quite understood that car. So when the Shadow convertible came along, I traded.

But the Subaru had one very redeeming feature: traction. It had a symmetrical all-wheel-drive set up that made it the best winter car I have known. It even beat the Jeep Cherokee we had for a while. Once, at the beginning of winter, I went zipping around the church parking lot in the Subaru to get my "slippery road bearings," and try as I might, I could not make that car fishtail. It stuck to the ground like there was special snow glue on the tires. It really had traction.

Traction is what Christians need. We need to hug the ground, all of us together, and not go fishtailing around. We need to stay focused and reach our destinations, becoming solid followers of Jesus and introducing others to Him. Slippery surfaces are inevitable, but with the right set-up we can hold the road too.

How do we do that? Like the Subaru, we need for every wheel to do its part, to turn at the right speed for the conditions we encounter. That happens when Christians do the basics well: Bible study, prayer, fellowship and sharing faith. It isn't complicated. It does require some discipline. It always works.

Life is a wild ride. We are much better off if we stay on the road than if we explore the ditch.

VIRGIN BIRTH

"Now the birth of Jesus Christ was like this: His mother, Mary, was discovered to be pregnant by the Holy Spirit ... " (Matthew 1:18).

I can imagine the angel Gabriel, given the task of explaining first to Mary and then to Joseph what was going to happen, and looking rather ashen, if that is possible for an angel, and saying to the Almighty, "They are never going to believe this. And even if Mary and Joseph do believe because of their wonderful child-like faith, the rest of the world will not get it." And I can imagine God replying, "Don't worry. I'll have Matthew and Luke write it very plainly for the rest of the world."

And so, Matthew, a former tax man and schooled in hard realities, took pains to note that the pregnancy was "*before* [Mary and Joseph] had sexual relations," and that Joseph himself wasn't too sure of the miraculous nature of the pregnancy until visited by Gabriel in a dream. And Matthew wrote that Gabriel used an Old Testament prophecy from Isaiah to help Joseph understand what was happening. The prophecy contained the term "virgin." Matthew also noted that after the dream, Joseph did not have sexual relations with Mary until *after* Jesus was born.

Then Luke, a medical doctor who knew about babies, and who was careful to look into things, and is known for accurate descriptions, wrote how Gabriel came to Mary and told her that she would "become pregnant and bear a son ... after the Holy Spirit came upon her" (Luke 1:31, 35). It is mysterious, but it is plain.

It needed to be plain because it was a one-of-a-kind occurrence. Some people think that is reason enough to dismiss the virgin birth. But every person on the planet is a one-of-a-kind occurrence. Each person has unique DNA, fingerprints, retinal patterns, and heat signatures. Even "identical" twins are not completely identical. So there is ample evidence of one-of-a-kind occurrences.

God was good enough to say why He was sending this baby in such a way. It has to do with Jesus' name. His name means "rescue" or "salvation." He came to rescue the world from sin. And only God can do such a thing. People cannot fix their own sinfulness. They may regret sin or excuse sin, but they cannot transform their hearts enough to become sinless. The birth of Jesus was an incarnation of God (that is to say God taking a body, or better said, God living as Himself and as a human being simultaneously) in order to fix sinfulness in people.

Jesus accomplished this by dying on a rough-hewn tree. Sin always costs something, usually the price of a damaged or shattered relationship. Jesus paid the price for everyone, rendering people "not guilty."

The virgin birth looked forward to Jesus' death on the cross so that salvation might be possible. All that is needed is enough faith to receive God's gift. When there is no faith, there is a gift not opened. There is a rescue not taken.

Jesus' subsequent resurrection from the dead was as unexpected as was the manner of His birth, but it is well attested. Paul knew of "more than five hundred of the brothers" who had seen Jesus all at one time after He rose from the dead, "most of whom [were] still living" at the time he was writing (1 Corinthians 15: 6).

All the other too-good-to-be-true messages in our world are just that. But the virgin birth is genuine. God had eyewitnesses write it out plainly in the pages of the Bible so we would get it. He is eager that we get it, because He loves us and our salvation depends upon it.

G.K. Chesterton wrote, "Christianity has not been tried and found wanting, but it has been found difficult [especially the believing part] and so not tried."

WE ALWAYS WIN

In the early part of September 2008, our church was part way through a building and remodeling project. Steve, one of the carpenters, was demolishing an old stairway to the lower level. The new stairway had been installed earlier that day in another location, with temporary treads on the new stringers until construction was completed. Workmen were going to be up and down on the new stairs, hauling out dirt and chunks of concrete, so it didn't make any sense to put the good treads on yet. As Steve pried the treads off the old stairway and knocked loose the old stringers, he explained the construction methods used in previous decades.

"See this old stringer on the side near the wall?"

I nodded.

"You can see how they cut the steps out of the board."

There were nice triangular spaces where the saw had done its work.

"Now look at this center stringer," he said. "The carpenters took all the little triangles and nailed them onto a two-by-four to make this middle stringer and conserve material." And so they had.

Steve continued to work at the old staircase. He was good with a crowbar. He had once worn one out knocking stucco off a house that needed to be redone.

"This is good old construction," he noted. The side stringers had been bolted to the concrete wall. Carpet on the steps had been nailed every inch so it wouldn't creep.

"But we always win," he added with a grin. "Eventually we knock down what we don't want and haul it out."

The Apostle Paul, who apparently had a lot of what he didn't want in his life by way of bad attitudes and behaviors, took the time to write about his frustration in his letter to his friends in Rome, Italy.

"I obviously need help!" he penned in Romans 7:15-25. "I realize that I don't have what it takes. I can will it, but I can't *do* it. I decide to do good, but I don't *really* do it; I decide not to do bad, but then I do it anyway. My decisions, such as they are, don't result in actions. Something has gone wrong deep within me and gets the better of me every time.

"It happens so regularly that it's predictable. The moment I decide to do good, sin is there to trip me up. I truly delight in God's commands, but it's pretty obvious that not all of me joins in that delight. Parts of me covertly rebel, and just when I least expect it, they take charge.

"I've tried everything and nothing helps. I'm at the end of my rope. Is there no one who can do anything for me? Isn't that the real question?" (*The Message*).

Paul's frustration is mine too, and perhaps yours. There is some awfully good old construction inside of us. Sinful construction. Awful construction. And solidly in there. Some days I ask along with Paul, "Is there no one who can do anything for me?"

As it turns out, there is someone. Paul found what he needed. No, he didn't look deep within himself to find some hidden strength. Or find a guru who knew the secrets of the universe and the key to his personal battle. He summed it up this way: "The answer, thank God, is that Jesus Christ can and does do something for me. He acted to set things right in this life of contradictions where I want to serve God with all my heart and mind, but am pulled by the influence of sin to do something so totally different."

Sometimes the progress is slow. Sometimes the quarters are cramped. Sometimes there are setbacks or things to puzzle out. But Jesus, with His Crowbar of Mercy, keeps at it until all that we don't want is knocked down and hauled out. And the good news is that He always wins. His crowbar never wears out. Which means we always win too, if we let Him do His work.

WET CEMENT

Mark chapter 13 is about the signs of the end of the age.

Jesus and His disciples are walking through the temple, and one of His friends remarks on the beauty of the architecture. To which Jesus responds that it will all be torn down in the not too distant future. (In 70 A.D. the Roman general Titus did destroy the city of Jerusalem after a four year siege, and the temple with it.) Jesus and His friends walk down through the Kidron Valley and up the Mount of Olives, where they sit down and look back at the city. Privately four of the friends ask Jesus to tell them what signs will accompany the fulfillment of His words.

Jesus explains that false Christs will arise and deceive people, wars will break out and rumors of wars will circulate, nations will struggle against each other, there will be earthquakes and famines and persecutions. The gospel will be preached to all countries, family members will betray each other and have each other put to death, and Christians will be hated by all men.

Then, starting with "an abomination which causes desolation" (from other Scriptures this would likely be the Antichrist, standing on the temple grounds and demanding worship in God's stead) a Great Tribulation will begin. Jesus tells Peter, James, John and Andrew that there has never been anything like this Tribulation, nor will there ever be anything like it again. In the distress of those days false prophets will appear and perform miraculous signs in an attempt to deceive and sway believers.

The Book of Revelation describes the Great Tribulation in more detail, using graphic apocalyptic language. And at the same time that the Antichrist is tormenting the world, God will pour out judgments, as seven scrolls are opened in heaven and seven angels blow their trumpets and seven more angles dump bowls of wrath upon the earth.

Thankfully there is good news about the end of the age too. Jesus goes on to explain that after the distress of those days, when "the sun is darkened and the moon does not give its light and the stars fall from the sky," then the Son of Man will appear, "coming in the clouds with great power and glory." This is not the very end, but the start of everything, in anticipation of a final showdown between the forces of good and evil.

Many people have studied the signs and events of the end of the age as Scripture presents them, and have undertaken to map out a sequence that best fits what we know. The ideas all have long, hard to pronounce names. The ideas vary and are in conflict with each other, and their proponents are quite sure that they have it right, and that their theological rivals, while brothers and sisters in the Lord, are also idiots. Which they probably are in the literal sense of the term. That is, they are completely occupied with themselves and their own ideas and have difficulty relating to those outside themselves.

Some think believers will be raptured and taken up to heaven with Christ before the Great Tribulation. Others think the Church will have to go through some or all of the Tribulation. Despite the absolute sufficiency of each position in the minds of the proponents, they all must admit that some Scriptures favor each position, and while each has a measure of plausibility (be it small or large), none is definitive.

My thought about the end of the age is that God, for His own reasons, has not given us every piece of information. Rather, He has given us pieces of a puzzle, but not all the pieces. And we have tried to force them into a picture without having all of them. Someday we will have them all and we will be able to say, "Oh, so that's how it is." And "Now I understand what was meant by that description in God's word."

While others are setting ideas in cement and letting them cure into solid positions, I prefer to let the cement be a little wet, so that I can still work it. As time unfolds, I expect things will come clear. But I don't figure I know it all now.

That doesn't make me popular with those who think they have the right sequence and interpretation of events to come. It just makes me maddeningly flexible.

WHAT I DO NOT LIKE

What I do not like about the week before deer season is the misgiving about where I have placed my stand. It is already in an excellent spot, on the side of a hill, overlooking a valley, near a couple different trails, with a good view and no real obstructions. I usually take a walk around the week before the opener, to see if anyone else has located a stand near mine, so I can be aware of where my shots are going and where shots might be coming from. But while doing so, invariably I find three or four more situations that seem better suited to a stand than where I have placed mine.

One year I walked back on a trail to the east of my current location. I thought I might set up just off the trail with a view in both directions, not far from some deer paths crossing on the perpendicular. The deer could easily slip behind where I am now and get into another part of the woods. If I set up off this other trail I could catch them by surprise. Then I walked a little further and realized that I could put a stand against a large birch tree where three trails meet. From there I can peer into a climax forest without much undergrowth. I did see a big doe there once.

I ambled down another path and found a newly formed pond and thought surely deer must come there to drink and if I sit opposite the pond I will see the Big Buck.

Finally, I was looping around some distance behind my stand, and found three large trees together. They were among sheltering hemlocks that would break up my silhouette, near a woodsy funnel. I thought this must be the best place. And I could always hunker down in the hemlocks to get out of the wind.

What to do, stay put or move? Leave the stand the deer are used to seeing or introduce a novel feature into the landscape? Or do deer even notice when you move something?

It occurs to me that the Evil One, God's Enemy and ours, wants us to go through a similar struggle with our Christian faith and values. He has various powers to influence people, but the chief tools in his bag are Doubt, Deception and Dissatisfaction. If he can get us to *doubt* what God has already revealed to us, or if he can *deceive* us into thinking God's take on reality is off somehow, or if he can cause us to become *dissatisfied* with what we have or who we are, he can be quite successful in his plan to lead us into sin, and in his plan to ruin us. I remember Pastor David Johnson, from the Church of the Open Door in Maple Grove, Minnesota, telling other pastors at a retreat, "Just because you start out well, doesn't mean you will end well." Then he told the story of Samson, who had all kinds of godly, spiritual "juice" but some fatal character flaws. Samson *doubted* God would remove his strength, though it was revealed to him that he must not cut his hair; he was *deceived* about the intentions of the lovely doe named Delilah, though God had given him several reality checks about her; and he was *dissatisfied* with the special vows he was under to God from his birth, and did not keep them. So he could not keep his favored role as God's judge over Israel. Departing from what he knew to be right cost him his ministry and his life.

What we know, by way of God's word and God's Spirit, we need to hold firm. We need to stay put in our trust and in our good values. Confidence in the right stuff is better than continual wondering about questionable stuff.

So ... in light of this spiritual revelation, I left my deer stand where it was, remembering that every year I see deer from it. And I shot a nice fork horn buck.

WHAT I LEARNED FROM MY FRONT PORCH

A mentor once cautioned me, "Don't run out of home projects." Presumably this was to insure my usefulness to the home and keep a roof over my head. When I got married, I had it made, since my wife came with a "honey do" list. She came with the kind of list that automatically re-supplies as projects are completed. One was putting a new deck on the front porch.

After mulling it over for a couple months I thought I had a fair idea of how to go about it. But as the thing unfolded, you'd think I had been reading *Recipes for Disaster* or *Murphy's Law Made Easy*, instead of the *Readers' Digest Book of Home Improvements*.

We decided to use that pretend wood, made mostly out of plastic, which is maintenance-free and lasts a long time. Our porch is a little over twenty feet long, so we bought twenty-foot long boards and planned to add perpendicular boards like bookends at either end. We could have had them delivered, but when I found I could save twenty dollars by renting a truck and hauling them myself, I did that. They were tied down in three places. But that stuff is slippery, and when I was five blocks from home, rolling carefully to a stop at the light in town ... If I ever do the back porch, I'm having them delivered.

So we had this scraped up new decking ready to screw down, most of which would look okay when there was thick fog. And I proceeded to tear off the old decking and replace it with the new. I did it a little at a time so I could do it myself and so we had enough of the porch still there for the newspaper man and the mailman during the project. There were some empty spaces between joists but I covered them with CDX. (Note to do-it-yourselfers: CDX of a certain length does not support the weight of a man. And the length is pretty short. Additional note: Having cut old decking with the sawzall in preparation for tearing it off, do not step on it. Cut decking does not support the weight of a man.)

There was a side project. The steps needed replacing too. So I made another trip to the home center and got more pretend wood. In short enough lengths to fit *inside* our van.

Replacing the steps was tricky. Four old steps came out. Five new ones went in. And five out of four people have trouble with fractions. I am one of the five. But my stepfather-in-law happened by and together we figured it out. I wanted facing on the stringers, and in my excitement over doing the math for the stringers themselves, I forgot to allow the proper overhang on the treads. Fortunately my friend, Jim, saw my dilemma. "Just move the treads out a little," he said. "What about the screws being in the wrong place and missing the stringers?" I asked. "Use the boards with screws already in them for the facing and cut new boards for the treads," he offered. It worked. A little modification of the railing, and we had a new porch. And I learned a valuable lesson: a person shouldn't try to do everything alone.

Twenty centuries ago King Solomon wrote in Proverbs 17:17, "... a brother is born for adversity." In other words, other people are there to help when things become difficult. It is not a sign of weakness to let others carry a slippery burden or help you watch your step or lend their math skills or show you an easier way. It is a sign of intelligence and humility.

And it is even more important to receive help from God. In *Uncommon Prayer*, Kenneth Swanson notes that some folks refuse to pray because they do not want help, even from God. It is a control thing. The truth is we cannot do some things for ourselves. We cannot work our own salvation. We cannot effectively face all of life's challenges with just our own resources.

God is not a magical genie waiting to grant wishes when we rub the prayer lamp, but He is a Good Friend, eager to have a deep friendship with those who will trust His ways. The kind of help He gives is not so much getting people out of jams as it is showing them how to live, which in turn is a help for avoiding a lot of jams and personal injury.

It is not always easy to ask for help. But it is usually wise. That old saying about God helping those who help themselves ... isn't in the Bible. It isn't even true. He helps those who know they need help, who know they need Him. And that's what I learned from my front porch.

WHEN ALL ELSE FAILS

When adventure is about to break over Spiderman, his spider sense makes him tingle. Northlanders experience something like that when big snow is coming. People who have things with cylinders in their garage tingle with anticipation. I was tingling that Saturday night in February on the eve of a big snow. I have a snow blower with a cylinder in my garage. I don't know why it seems more like an adventure than work to blow out the driveway. It just does.

It is a Craftsman snow blower with a Tecumseh engine, which I bought in the summer at a garage sale. I had the folks put gas in it and start it up, and I watched it crawl and spin the auger. The price was right, so I took it home and waited.

Sunday morning found me in the garage tingling and grinning. I set the choke, pushed the throttle to "run" and pulled the starter cord. It came off in my hand. Old cord. No problem. Half an hour later it was reunited with the recoil unit and I pulled again. The recoil unit failed. The spring had detached from whatever it is usually attached to. I was crestfallen. Fortunately, I have a neighbor with a monster snow blower who takes pity on me. He tingled and grinned all up and down my driveway.

I took the offending part to a repair shop the next week. The owner looked for another unit. He didn't have one. He took a closer look and decided to try and fix mine. This was followed by comments, not all favorable, about the design and construction, and by searching for the right iron punch and hammer to knock out the bushing, and by dropping a small spring on the floor and stepping on it, and, with the aid of needle-nose pliers he really didn't like, setting the detached spring right again. He wound a little tension into the recoil unit before putting it all together. Exactly how much tension is a trade secret. He told me this with a menacing look as he concealed what he was doing.

But the repair shop owner did let me watch some of the work. While I was there in his inner sanctum he got several phone calls, sometimes talking on two phones at once. I had a few minutes to look over the tools on his bench and the ones hanging on the pegboard. There were tools I had never seen before, like a curved-handle crescent wrench and some I can't describe that were marked "for authorized personnel only." I can't describe them because I think he sprayed me with gas that made me forget most of what I saw. But I do remember the one he saved as a last resort. Hanging at the top of one pegboard was a hand grenade. It was harmless, the bottom having been drilled and the explosive stuff removed. But I thought, "This is what you turn to when all else fails. If you can't fix it, you blow it up!"

I am always pleased when something is made to work again after being broken. I admire the repair shop owner who knows how to restore broken machines. Thanks to him, my snow blower works. He reminds me that God restores people to life after they have been broken. And being really good at this, God never has a day of frustration so great that He reaches for a hand grenade. He has no "when all else fails" tool. The flood came close, but he had an "ark tool" by which he salvaged Noah and his family and restored the whole world.

We, of course, have grenades of various descriptions. We resort to divorce, abuse, running away, suicide and some lesser expressions of anger and frustration. What we cannot fix, we often blow up. Often the most difficult thing is to put the broken parts of our lives into God's hands. Maybe the reason is that, since Adam and Eve broke their relationship with God in the Garden of Eden, we have tried to hide the broken parts, or fix them ourselves, as if we were God. We can hide, cope or make do, but only God can fix what is severely broken in us.

The Old Testament prophet Isaiah wrote "Surely the arm of the LORD is not too short to save" (Isaiah 59:1). God Himself has been hurt and broken, despised, rejected, ignored and misunderstood. In the person of Jesus He was killed. Or better said, He willingly laid down His life. He took on the world's brokenness, and paid with His own life to get it fixed. That is the story of Good Friday. Then, when Jesus was raised from the dead, something new happened. What had been un-fixable—namely death—suddenly became fixable. That is the story of Easter. If death is fixable, then everything else is fixable too. If not in this life, then in the next one, for those who trust in Jesus. The cross and the empty tomb are the ultimate tools. They grab hold of a person's faith and fix any kind of brokenness. Even when all else fails.

WHY EVIL HAS NOT OVERWHELMED THE WORLD

We should not kid ourselves. There is plenty of evil in the world. War, racism, poverty, prejudice, greed, terrorism, illness and famine all testify to this uncomfortable truth. Another uncomfortable truth, which accounts for evil, though many would argue the point, is that people are not basically good. The theological way of saying it, is that we live in a "fallen world" and each of us "trips and falls" to some extent. If we are honest, we will admit this is so, even though the humanists say people and conditions are improving all the time. It really is more accurate to say that the world is "going to hell in a hand basket." Still, it has not gotten there yet. Why not?

One reason that evil is held somewhat in check is that a small number of people make heroic efforts on behalf of good. In their own spheres of influence, whether local or global, these people wage fierce battles against moral destruction, and show by example what good looks like. People like Brother Andrew, who used to smuggle Bibles behind the Iron Curtain. He now works for peace in the Middle East by bringing Jewish Christians and Palestinian Christians together.

Because of their common bond in Christ, conflicts about race and about homeland (each huge in itself) are being overcome. But it is terribly difficult work as you might imagine.

Another reason that evil does not take over the world is that a large number of people live with simple integrity and sound values, holding back the surge of evil the way a dam holds back floodwaters. The Church Universal has always been a force for good and a force that restrains evil in the world. People, transformed by Jesus, make an enormous difference with love for Him which then results in love for neighbors. Obedience to laws, care for the marginalized, fairness and selflessness, hard work, the appreciation of beauty, thankfulness, confession of shortcomings, reconciliation with others and prayers of intercession all keep wickedness at bay and promote the general well-being.

Though we don't often see them, angels account for some of the victories against evil too. Corrie ten Boom, who survived a Nazi concentration camp, spent time in Vietnam, during the conflict there, visiting hospitals and telling wounded soldiers about Jesus. One night the hospital where she was visiting was threatened with a Viet Cong attack, and the staff and patients prayed diligently for safety. The next morning, while spending time with a wounded Viet Cong soldier being treated by our allies, she asked why his unit had not launched an attack. "We could not," he told her, "because of all the soldiers in white." There were no special forces in white uniforms in that area. Corrie and those with her came to understand that they had been protected by angels. Evil cannot work when there is supernatural protection.

There are also certain spiritual principles at work in the world by God's design. One is that good triumphs over evil. An analogy is that when you open a closet door, light from the room pours in and illumines the closet. Darkness does not pour out of the closet and darken the room. Good, which comes from God's character, is stronger than evil, which stems from the devil's character. It is the devil's character over which human beings "trip and fall" when evil gains ground.

A final consideration is that evil people find it difficult to organize. They do sometimes, as the Holocaust and other similar events in history remind us. But evil is often thwarted by disorganization and by suspicion among the workers of evil. Many secret societies and many with a thirst for power have aimed at dominating the world.

Occasionally they have come close. But none has been completely successful. My father-in-law explained their failure quite succinctly when he said, "Nuts just can't work together."

The Bible says that someday things will get much worse than they are now. World events will move toward a final showdown between good and evil, between God and His enemies. The Bible also says that God will win, that good will succeed, that justice will prevail, all of which gift us with wonderful hope. And, motivation to be on the right side when it happens.

PART II
THROUGH ANNE'S REARVIEW MIRROR

THE WRITE TIME

"The use of the right word, the exact word, is the difference between a pencil with a sharp point and a thick crayon."
　　　　　　Peter Marshall

It was the fall of 1977, the first semester of my senior year at the University of Wisconsin-Madison. The campus was both stunningly spectacular and spectacularly stunning in autumn. A common ailment among the college students was a prolonged case of sensory overload as we tried to process the candy-apple red and pumpkin orange colors of the sugar maple leaves dressing the trees lining Bascom Hill, bicycle tires crunching the gravel on the lake shore path, the sun shimmering on Lake Mendota in shards of crystal, the magnificent scent of crisp, still air. (That may be unique to the Midwest. I'm not sure people in other parts of the country understand how the air can simply *smell* like autumn, even without wood smoke, but Wisconsinites know that somehow it just does.) I would not have willingly chosen to leave campus for fifteen weeks—from the most splendid part of September through the snowiest part of December—for any other reason than my student teaching experience.

I wanted to work with children since my teen years and waded through six previous semesters of numerous American and British Literature classes, Social Disorganization (it seemed like college students already excelled in that), Astronomy, Calculus, British History, Philosophy, Sociology, several Elementary Education classes for both regular education and special education, Shakespeare, Communicative Disorders, Linguistics, even Badminton. It was finally my chance to finish with the shallower water and swim in over my head. I was nervous and excited at the thought that student teaching would be my toughest course in the real, hopefully delightful, sometimes gritty lives of children. My transcript at the end of that semester would record only twelve credits; although normally considered a part-time status, (I had taken fifteen to nineteen credits every other semester) this would count as full-time for a student teacher. Those twelve credits would be earned Monday through Friday, seven-thirty to four-thirty in a fourth grade class at John F. Kennedy Elementary School in Madison.

By the end of my first day in the classroom, I realized that my supervising teacher was superb: Patient, engaging, gifted, and highly skilled at firm, kind classroom management. Every day in Mrs. Hawley's "learning lab" was a joyful, challenging one. I considered myself blessed to have her for a mentor as much as the children obviously did to have her as their teacher. And, unlike several of my college classmates whose student teaching experiences were heavy on grading papers and being aides for the troubled students, my days were filled with actual teaching: reading, math, science and social studies. I looked for every opening to slip music into the classroom as well, but breathed an audible sigh of relief when I discovered that I would not be expected to give art instruction. That would have been a certain deal-breaker for me and maybe even resulted in my "flunking" student teaching.

So far, so good—until the day arrived when I was forced to attempt a drawing on the board to illustrate a lesson. I do not remember either the picture or the lesson: The brain works in survival mode and tends to block harmful memories. My students were undoubtedly expecting to be dazzled by yet another hidden talent from their creative student teacher, whatever the illustration may have been.

My hand guided a seemingly reluctant, thin taper of institutional-white chalk quietly across a familiar expanse, as if the chalk itself were careful not to squeal, desperately trying to distance itself from the artistic crime about to be committed.

I turned around and saw my favorite student timidly raising her hand.

"Yes, Lynnette?"

"Miss Colvin, you don't need to try to make us feel better by drawing bad."

My student teacher status was set to plunge into the depths of young-and-single-but-no-longer-cool, even while my mind automatically changed Lynnette's "bad" into "badly." I made a mental note to re-teach adverbs while considering how to pull up before crashing my self-esteem. My ten year-olds held their breath, wondering whether I would reprimand Lynnette for being disrespectful. I stared at thirty sets of vulnerable eyes openly displaying fear, and knew that the high road of painful honesty was the only path available to me. "I'm actually drawing the best I can!" The resulting explosion of laughter would, I hoped, reinstate my status and reveal the imperfections of adults, all within an accepting environment.

This was the anti-climax of years of my trying and failing to learn any kind of art: drawing, painting and sculpting, sketching, shading, daubing, glossing, glazing or firing. Fresco and deco, pigments and prisms and tones were not in my wheel house, were barely even in my vocabulary.

I did eventually perfect one kind of art: a kaleidoscope of excuses to keep me out of any party game involving drawing, particularly "Pictionary". As a natural extrovert, it was unnatural for me to be a bystander, but the potential for embarrassment forced me into a state of temporary introvertism. Introvertitis. Introversion. I was resigned to the reality that I was not a member of the club of people who mysteriously turn a block of clay into an oil lamp; who know how to use water colors or acrylics or charcoal to transform a piece of paper into a sunset, a classic car, a skyline.

I wondered why our Heavenly Father with a deep and wide gene pool did not choose a strand of artistry to program into my DNA. It took decades for me to understand that my deficiency was not in my hands but in my mind, where I constantly tripped over my narrow definition of art, blind to the gift God had lovingly lavished on me. I now see clearly that my artistry exists in words: Nouns and adjectives and adverbs and sometimes even split infinitives are my medium, and I brush stroke them across the canvas of a blank page to paint a self-portrait. I can also sculpt a biography, sketch an essay or fire a challenge. The tools of my craft are a box of sharpened, colored words, a bottle of fluid thoughts, prisms of ideas, tones of emotion, shades of contemplation and the glaze of truth.

My essays come in a spectrum-spanning diversity of humor and thoughtfulness, encouragement and discomfort. They have evolved out of my life experiences, which make some complete and leave others a work-in-progress; these are explored in the essay "Spare Parts" near the end of the book.

Oliver Wendell Holmes said that a mind stretched to a new idea never returns to its original shape. After reading these essays you may discover an elastic thought. The back of the book has pages with only titles. Each of them awaits your hand at filling in the canvas. You may want to draw conclusions, color outside the box of expectations, shade an opinion or paint a scene. Do not gloss over your artistic endowment, the inheritance from your Father. There is a write time for the right occasion and a right time for the write circumstance. Choose your tool and explore your artistry.

AN ECONOMY OF WORDS

"The Word is the verb, and the verb is God."
Victor Hugo

"In the beginning was the **WORD**": God. Creator. Provider. Lover. Abba.
"And the **WORD** was with God": Jesus. Logos. Emmanuel. Shepherd. Savior.
"And the **WORD** was God" : Spirit. Comforter. Intercessor. Convicter.

"Let there be light!" Darkness scattered.

"Where are you?" Exposed Rebellion. Planned Redemption.

"I AM." God is. Forever.

"Moses! Moses!" Sacred call.

"Thou shalt not steal." Protective command.

"Seek justice." Mercy reigns.

"I AM The Door." The Forever Way to God.

"Fear not." Love seeks His own.

"You are the Christ." Confession. Understanding.

"Jesus wept." Humanity-wrapped Divinity.

"Be still!" Creation subdued.

"Follow me." Challenge. Uncertainty. Trust.

"It is finished!" Perfect work.

"Let the words of my mouth and the meditation of my heart
be acceptable in Your sight, O Lord, my Rock and my Redeemer."

Psalm 19:14 (NAS)

"I wait for the Lord, my soul does wait, and in His WORD do I hope."

Psalm 130:5 (NAS)

COURT IS (NOT) IN SESSION

I am drawn to fictional courtroom attorneys. Though not wired for politics, I envy the lawyers depicted in novels by John Grisham and in TV shows like "Law and Order," because the lawyers say all of the things I wish I had either thought of or had the courage to say in the middle of personal arguments which generated more heat than light, more emotion than substance. Lawyers are "last-word" characters to whom everyone and everything in the courtroom is required to listen. I can imagine even the walls holding their breath while the pictures and plaques hang at attention. Who has been left unmoved after watching Gregory Peck portray Atticus Finch in "To Kill a Mockingbird?" His incredible closing argument, even though it carries no weight on a bent scale of prejudice, always reduces me to tears.

I am also pulled into the drama of juries. When jurors exit a courtroom to begin their deliberation, the atmospheric pressure rises to a clammy tension. If the jury, meanwhile, encased in a windowless, artificial world, indulges in man's tendency toward pre-determined opinion, the result becomes the powerful "Twelve Angry Men," a 1957 movie adapted from an earlier teleplay which catapulted Jack Warden, Jack Klugman, Lee J. Cobb, John Fiedler, Robert Webber and Martin Balsam into famous acting careers. (Henry Fonda was the dissenting juror and already a megastar.)

Lawyer movies and novels have reached critical mass in our culture, whether because of the drama I have described, or because we need attorneys to be our GPS across the unfamiliar territory of mortgages, foreclosures, child support, boundary disputes and lawsuits of every shape and size. It is plausible, then, that legal drama, whether the stuff of movies or the real framework of our lives, has taken on a new life form in our churches. Pastors morph into lawyers expected to deliver convincing Opening and Closing arguments for the most contentious cases. One of these is the correct defense of Genesis, the Opening of God's Word and world. In the Beginning ... how did God create the world? How long did He take to do it? Is there an acceptable marriage of science and faith? If the lawyer presents the best case, usually one that validates our previously-held beliefs, then the jurors will find in his favor. The same holds true for the lawyer's Closing argument: How does he present the book of Revelation, specifically the End times and Rapture? When and how will the Rapture take place, and what about the Tribulation? Are there exhibits A and B which include the most popular theologian or author of the day?

The congregation sits as jury, although seldom an impartial one. Jurists who enter the courtroom bring experiences through which they filter the lawyer's words. And in the same way that juries leave a courtroom for deliberation, people may leave the church, then re-enter and try to persuade the rest of the jury into holding their opinions. Sometimes the juries try for new counsel if they perceive that the lawyer does not present strong enough evidence for a particular case, or if there is potential for a hung jury which would add to the stress of contentious relationships.

*****

Could we assemble a team of impartial jurors from outside the walls of our church? In our judicial system, this is the goal; in our churches, is a team of neutral people more desirable than one holding pre-determined views? If people enter the sanctuary and are not partial to the issues presented by the pastor and deliberated by the congregation, perhaps the issues hold no relevance to their lives. Are we "trying" issues not on the docket of eternity?

*****

The church is the Courtroom of the King but one without lawyers, juries, or even self-appointed judges of biblical interpretation. The New Testament model of the Church does not portray pastors as lawyers; they are proclaimers, teachers, prophets, shepherds, servants, vessels of vulnerability. Worshipers are not jurors; they are leaders, deacons, accountants, servers, encouragers, revelators of Truth. Neither pastor nor congregation is equipped with the gavel of judgment; that is reserved solely for The Righteous Judge.

May we hang a "Gone Fishing" sign above our doors and become fishers of men, a redemptive and biblical model of the Church.

LEND ME YOUR EAR

I have no navigational system in the world of drawing, painting and sculpting. (I do not even like to wield a brush or roller to paint the walls in my house.) When I visited New York City thirty years ago, I did not tour the Museum of Modern Art. I am unfamiliar with famous painters and their work, although I have at least heard of Rembrandt, Picasso and Van Gogh. I know that Vincent Van Gogh painted "The Starry Night" thanks to the '70's song by Don McLean, and that he painted pictures with big, brightly colored flowers. But since I am interested in people's life stories, when I hear Van Gogh's name my mind immediately travels not to his sunflower painting but to "that troubled guy who cut off part of his ear."

Why is Van Gogh's partial ear loss more compelling than if he had lost a big toe in an accident? Is it because any kind of facial disfigurement is far more personal than the loss of a digit? I wonder why he chose partial ear loss over, say, toe loss. Was hearing less valuable than walking?

There is a man in the Bible who lost his entire ear, but not through self-infliction. During the last Thursday of Jesus' life, in the evening, He prayed in the Garden of Gethsemane with His eyes open, staring into the face of the fullness of time. As Judas gave Jesus the kiss of betrayal, His disciple Peter (the same one who betrayed Jesus less than twenty-four hours later) drew a sword and struck the slave of the high priest, cutting his ear completely off. (Although this story is recorded in all four Gospels, only John names both Peter and Malchus, the slave. We learn that Jesus healed Malchus' ear only from the Gospel of Luke.) It is possible that otherwise biblically illiterate people have somehow heard about the man in the Bible who suffered the loss of his ear through violence. Once again, there is something that draws us to stories about harm to the face. Why did Peter choose to cut off Malchus' ear rather than his arm, which would have greatly disabled him as a slave, perhaps costing him his livelihood?

There is nothing more recorded about Malchus. I feel fortunate to be able to attach a name to this Passion Week event, because so many minor people who played a major role in the Bible remain nameless. The Samaritan woman at the well had a life-changing encounter with Jesus, yet we never discover her name, the names of her husbands, or the rest of her journey. Such is also true for the woman caught in adultery; we read neither her name nor how her life unfolds after she meets Jesus, and we are left with more questions than answers. What we know for sure is that she is arguably the most famous woman in the New Testament. The Old Testament records judges, the Shunammite widow helped by Elisha, various prophets—all people who walked across the stage, spoke their lines, became a footnote in the script of history, and returned to obscurity.

Back to Malchus, who became an ear-witness to the healing power of Jesus: Did he wear his scar proudly? Did he change teams and decide to follow the teachings of this God-Man? Did he leave his position as slave of the high priest and become servant of the High Priest Jesus?

I have filled multiple journals over the past thirty-five years, but I do not assume that anyone else is recording the events of my life. It is doubtful that my name will even be remembered four generations from now. But my name is not a requirement for leaving an inkblot on the page of another's life. People are watching and listening today, maybe pondering what will happen if my physical hearing decreases with an increase in age, or if my face becomes disfigured through stroke or illness. Though nameless, I may be the one to point someone to the Master Healer before I exit stage left.

LITERALLY SPEAKING

Each generation of Christians seems to have a litmus test that separates the haves of genuine faith from the have-nots of cultural Christmas-and-Easter religiosity. Some of these tests take the form of popular sayings eventually taken out of commission; one from my childhood was, "Don't smoke, don't chew, don't go with guys who do." (The American Cancer Society picked up the baton and now runs the race for healthier lifestyles.) "Don't be a back-pew Baptist" was another admonition. (Modern church buildings, or "worship centers," have retired sanctuary pews and replaced them with multi-purpose room chairs.)

"I take the Bible literally" is a statement with no expiration date, one that has been loudly and proudly proclaimed and disputed for several decades. The basic premise of taking the Bible literally is that it is read at face value, that it is God's truth, and that it is the best and only road map for our lives. In the vernacular of Minnesotans, "It's all good." A literal interpretation of the divinely inspired Word of God protects us from reading it like an ala carte menu and choosing what will be easiest to digest; or from choosing the comforting and comfortable stories while avoiding the ones that challenge us and defy all of the expected rules of engagement. There is no flying under the radar when God's Word confronts our spirit, shapes our attitude, informs our language and controls our tongue; it lays us bare before the One Who knows us deeply and still loves us dearly. The strength in taking the Bible literally is that we do not bring a politically-correct interpretation to the Word in order to change it; we understand that the Bible will change us, and that it will often be more like the pain of major surgery than the innocuous application of a band aid.

The fact that the word "literal" does not appear anywhere in the Bible is not problematic, because everyone understands what it means. Theology is in its place, the words mean exactly what they say, and our tightly woven garment of righteousness is never in any danger of fraying. There are no loose strings to accidentally pull, either by us, by someone else, or by a political agenda, even one from within the church.

My teaching-pastor husband recently challenged his congregation to look carefully at the word literal. Since I understand the significance of definitions, and of the search for the best word, I turned to an important tool in studying God's Word: a comprehensive dictionary, which I own in the form of The Oxford English Reference Dictionary, Revised Second Edition, containing 250,000 words, phrases and definitions, and published in 2002. The Oxford Dictionary defines literal as, "taking words in their usual or primary sense without metaphor or allegory." This is where the journey of faith becomes challenging. The Bible is a compilation of writing that is figurative, poetic, prophetic, allegorical, symbolic, historical, and musical, and not all literal in the dictionary definition which, if we abide by the strict definition, would require us to conclude, for instance, that God is a bird, since the Psalmist writes that He shelters us under the shadow of His wings. We know that this is a word picture of the protective nature of our Heavenly Father, which makes this passage symbolic rather than literal.

We are admonished in Second Timothy to accurately handle the word of truth. Perhaps we should create a new word and describe ourselves as *accurate-ists* rather than *literalists*. An accurate-ist would be a person committed to understanding the accuracy of Scriptural writing: the wisdom literature, apocryphal literature, parables, hyperbole, history, commands. The inspired, remarkable, dynamic Word of God was written over a time span of 1,400 years by poets, nomads, warrior kings, doctors, lawyers, rabbis, shepherds, beauty queens, prophets, fishermen, humble saints and outrageous sinners, each with a different personality and perspective to his or her writing. Not all were literal, but all were accurate.

If I take the Bible literally in my reading of First Corinthians chapter eleven, I would always have my head covered in church. I have not seen any head-coverings among the women in my congregation except on Easter Sunday and on cold northern Minnesota days. We are therefore all in danger of a biblical interpretation that is less than literal. An accurate reading of the Word, however, gives me the context of the Apostle Paul's admonition, in which he addressed gentile women new to the faith, former prostitutes marked by uncovered heads, and as such, women who brought disruption and chaos to a group of people struggling to find their new identities in Christ. The head covering was similar to a modern woman's wedding ring: It demonstrated restraint and faithfulness, and in that culture, it made room for peacefulness and order in worship. This is not an issue faced by twenty-first century American women, although there are denominations in which this passage is still interpreted literally and require the women to cover their heads during worship. A majority of believers do not interpret this passage literally, but understand instead that the purpose of Paul's admonition was to address a specific issue in a specific context. We can still, however, read this passage accurately and glean a basic principle of the need for all of us, both men and women, to be respectful during worship, and to refrain from dress or behavior that would be a stumbling block or distraction to our brothers and sisters in Christ.

*****

My earlier symbol of a literalist as a person wearing a tightly woven garment of righteousness could be changed to an accurate-ist wrapped in a patchwork quilt made with squares representing the variety of literature inspired by our multi-faceted God. This quilt could enfold the Church with the strength to withstand the stretching of the expected theological tugs-of-war on this side of eternity. Some of those battles involve the Apostle Paul's admonitions to the early church: Which should be read only literally? There are Christians trying to move issues out of the literal category into a culturally irrelevant one, and therein lies one of the most volatile issues of our day: Homosexuality is no longer defined as sin, which is so "last year," so "out of context" for today's believers, even though it is denounced multiple times in both the Old and New Testaments. This is why it becomes crucial that we understand the different types of writing within the Bible, not so that everything we previously defined as literal will become culturally irrelevant, but so that things can move in the other direction: Those issues currently defined as irrelevant will be properly understood as literally sinful. We cannot add to the growing pile of political correctness and cultural irrelevance simply because it is easier and less controversial to do so.

Let us be about the business of "working out our salvation with fear and trembling," with gentle humility, with the goal of unity, and with an accurate reading of the Word.

MR. POTATO HEAD

At the beginning of my marriage I was given one very practical piece of advice, a guaranteed antidote to hoarding: If I had not eaten, worn or otherwise used an item within six months, I should consider taking it out of its domesticated state and returning it to the wild via a rummage sale, charity or local landfill. The timeframe of six months was a bit too confining for my psyche, but I have indeed followed the basic formula, and my appetite for de-cluttering and simplifying has been fed.

I do, however, nourish a certain scope for imagination, as L. L. Montgomery's character in Anne of Green Gables ("Anne with an e", for which I am very grateful) so famously proclaimed. A life consistently unencumbered would neglect nostalgia, minimize memories, and become boringly barren. A sanitized house without personality would be all wood and windows, more like a police station or Division of Motor Vehicles than a place for people to mix and match words and emotions, easy chairs and difficult experiences.

My home embraces closet space for high school yearbooks, photo albums, hand-made quilts passed down through generations, journals, keepsakes that honor friends, value family and trigger memories. These are what transform a utilitarian, water-proof lean-to into the original meaning of comfort zone.

Even my garage shares responsibility for storing memories. There are multiple plastic bins filled with our adult children's favorite childhood toys and games: Lincoln Logs and Tinker Toys, Barbie Dolls and Legos, Matchbox cars and Beanie Babies. None of these things is battery co-dependent. All are guaranteed a long and healthy shelf-life, awaiting a call to service in the next generation of children.

One of my favorite toys is Mr. Potato Head. How has something so simple, so inexpensive, so non-electronic and anti-technological captured our imagination since its birth in the 1940s? Down through the generations he has morphed from a real potato body to a plastic torso, has acquired a wife, pet pals, and a galactic identity, yet Mr. Potato Head has maintained his original purpose: To offer a limited but strangely satisfying arrangement of his hat, nose, feet, ears and mustache. It never takes long to discover, however, that his parts can be assembled in anatomically incorrect and comical ways, and that becomes much more gratifying than simply placing the parts in their intended slots. I wonder what would happen if a social psychologist gathered two groups of adults in a room and asked one group to assemble Mr. Potato Head according to the boxed instructions while the other group indulged its sense of free-spirited assemblage. I bet the second group would snicker, swap parts, feel unbounded joy without really knowing why, and be the object of great envy by the compliant group.

It is possible that this uncomplicated childhood toy reveals something of our spiritual nature. We begin with basic parts: feet, arms, lips, hat and eyes. Each part has its own purpose in the Body of Christ: The feet spread God's grace; the arms embrace God's people; the lips proclaim God's goodness; the hat protects God's Word; the eyes identify God's poor.

Mr. Potato Head's parts are stored in the back flap of his torso for ease of assembly. All of the necessary parts are there. After all of the parts are inserted in their intended slots, Mr. Potato Head is good to go. In the same way, a believer's parts can be stored in one place, one church, and assembled as God-the-manufacturer intended. This, however, is way too ordinary for multitudes of believers. There just is not enough excitement in doing it that way. A far more circuitous and adventurous part-search often becomes its own end. The journey leads a believer first to a megachurch with rock-concert status for music appreciation, then to a neighborhood Bible study for spiritual growth, through a popular book for prophecy, next to a seminar or speaker for encouragement, and over, around, and through every brightly-burning church and para-church organization within the radius of the city and beyond. Assembling the parts is not expected, only endless accumulation without ever completing the body: A spiritual torso ready for inaction.

****

There *are* believers who gather a scattered set of parts and attempt to assemble them; the next step, then, requires a mirror to check the assembly. The book of James describes a man who looks at his reflection in a mirror, promptly walks away and immediately forgets what kind of person he is. This can happen when either a self-made person is not interested in being accountable to anyone else for how he looks, or when he does not trust the reflections from fellow believers whose mirrors are flawed—who struggle with gossip or incivility or jealousy or adultery—and so he gathers his parts and moves on to the next whistle stop. These self-contained believers feel satisfied and justified as nomadic part collectors.

How easily and recklessly we are deceived and end up looking like Mr. Picasso-Head, a torso with unidentifiable parts sticking out in disturbing disarray. Christians may hold up flawed mirrors before us, but they nevertheless encourage us to look at ourselves. Are the parts where they belong? Do they fit well? Have we tried to put two parts into the same slot? (Are we trying to talk and listen at the same time?) Does our body have ears but no arms or feet—hearing about needs but lacking the willingness to deliver a meal, load a moving van, or visit a person dealing with depression? Do we lack a hat—oblivious to the evil we allow into our heads? Are there lips where there should be eyes—words without compassion? Do we need to trade an extra set of lips—an abundance of gossip—for a set of arms to embrace those who ache?

There are plenty of opportunities in our soft-landing culture to enter a church, stay for a month, a year, a season, and never consider our reflection until we give an over-the-shoulder glance on the way out the door to the next place. It is also tempting to limit our friendship circle to a group of "hand-picked" mirrors who promise to reflect only our best and obscure our wrong choices. And, with our persuasiveness, that group of mirrors may travel with us as we make the church rounds within a community.

I may seem hopelessly naïve in my approach. (After all, I am married to a pastor and therefore cannot break ranks to attend a different church.) Or it may seem like I am elevating the attribute of perseverance in one church above all else. No. There are times when harshness or conceit or politically-correct but scripturally-incorrect theology can and should compel believers to leave a church in search of one that demonstrates a proper knowledge of God's Word and respect for His people. We are admonished in Scripture to exercise discernment, and there are mainstream churches in mainstream denominations that have reinterpreted God's Word until it exposes, rather than recreates, the culture, functioning as a thermometer rather than a thermostat. These are valid reasons for seeking a new body of believers committed to God's Truth.

There are, however, many Christians looking for a revolving door at the back of a church, taking the Mr. Potato Head approach to church attendance and opportunities for service. These people become obsessed over multiple parts gleaned from all of the most exciting churches and speakers and books and movements, resulting in an abundance of legs and arms and lips, an overflowing bucket of gifts without a place to pour themselves out in service. Sometimes they become self-appointed voices of righteousness to those whom they think are lacking the right parts. This does not build up the body and often brings divisiveness. Or, they might pick and choose their favorite parts and assemble them in a guarded, witness-protection-program kind of way, resulting in inadequate or imbalanced or incorrect function—in the belief that they are "doing ministry," without the confirmation and encouragement of the rest of the church.

My idea of balance is that we find our parts in one place, one church, assemble the parts there over a long time and trust our spiritual family to show us an accurate image of ourselves, even through scratched or cloudy mirrors. We are to strive for perfection, but will not attain it on this side of eternity. This is God's astounding plan for the spreading of His Kingdom; there is no Plan B.

Our ultimate goal is not simply to reflect each other's image and let that be the end, but that we reflect the character of our Heavenly Father in our lives, our words, our attitudes, the way we treat each other, how we look and what we say. The world is looking intensely at us. What we hope they will see is a humble and maturing group of believers, properly assembled, balanced, respectful, useful and ready to show grace and forgiveness to a world that needs to experience grace from the One Who is Grace Incarnate.

ONE SIZE FITS ALL

My favorite shopping spree involves books: fiction, non-fiction, biographies, classics, children's stories, out-of-print—treasures all. Clothes shopping, on the other hand, is a necessary non-spree; it is less energizing and more anxiety-provoking than the adventure of unearthing a book at a store, rummage sale or on the Internet. Books need to be a good match for my mind and heart but do not involve my body, while clothes shopping becomes a safari through the waist-land of self-esteem. I often need to ignore the numbers on the clothing tags and simply try on what looks like a good fit. I avoid the skirts and dresses from the one-size-fits-all racks, even though they are bright and attractive. I do not understand how one universal size is marketable given the reality that women do not share identical measurements and combinations of height, weight, shape, arm and leg length. With the exception of rain ponchos, many women wearing one-size-fits-all clothes walk around looking to me like they are distractedly tugging and tucking and coercing their cookie-cutter outfits into reluctant obedience to their unique figures. Only Dr. Seuss' sneetches could get away with wearing uni-clothes.

I see this clothes-shopping mentality in the church, where both women and men search for a place to worship that is tailor made and offers a flattering fit, a garment that highlights their best features and hides their faults. Congregations are tried on for size. Perhaps a desire for a high volume of people and excitement is tempered with the need for a close, tight-knit family of care-givers. Maybe music—the hot-button issue of the modern church—needs to blend power point techno worship with favorite childhood hymns, combining contemporary rock with hundreds of years of sacred music. Helping the poor and managing finances share importance with websites and satellite dishes.

Balance and variety in churches are a part of God's creativity and gifting, but that is not the same thing as people pushing their shopping carts throughout a city, trying on churches and walking around in them, pulling off the price tags of commitment and reattaching them to the elected leaders. The reasons for eventually rehanging churches on the discard rack are endless: They do not have the appropriate children's programs or youth groups; the Bible studies are too much Bible and not enough current authors; evangelism is scarce; there are too many formerly unchurched people who do not demonstrate acceptable behavior; the sermons are too long or too short, too loud or too quiet, too simplistic or overly mentally demanding; the service is too early, too late or not offered in an adequate number of time slots, too loud and charismatic or too mundane; the building is too warehouse-large, too red-brick small, too institutional-new, too moldy-old; too community-center utilitarian or too ornately antiquated; or, there are no easily identifiable issues, it just doesn't *feel* right. The one thing guaranteed to stick to the bottom of the shopping cart of an exiting believer is an unsettled spirit.

Disgruntled people determined to stay in the church and remain dissatisfied focus their efforts on unraveling the church garment theological thread by theological thread, hoping to re-knit it into a new, near-perfect fit. Pleasant people undecided about staying may ask: If I let go of the shopping cart and keep this garment, how will I deal with the embarrassment of those people whose words or actions add pulls and stains and wrinkles and puckers? My church will not be nearly as attractive as the one on the other side of town.

When a body of believers wears one garment it is often uncomfortable, and that is likely part of God's design. Sometimes it feels too tight when we are challenged to release resources or worship next to those who hold political and biblical views very different from ours. The practice of prayer and tongues and healing and Holy Spirit baptisms leaves some people with the sensation of wearing a garment that has been turned inside out. Arms of compassion may extend without restraint into the surrounding community; will the fabric withstand the stretch?

I do not find any instances in God's Word of tailor-made church. The book of Acts records the earliest body of believers who shared and sinned, appointed and delegated, embraced and taught, prayed and baptized, all with extravagance and gladness of heart. If we jump ahead two thousand years we find the entitlement mentality that drives many believers to expect and demand and endlessly search for a church that meets all of their criteria for flattery and comfort. God's Church is not an abundant, form-fitting wardrobe; it is a one-size-fits-all robe of righteousness ready to clothe His dressed-for-success but spiritually-naked world.

PASSIVE-AGGRESSIVE UNINSTALL

Passive aggressive is the catch phrase of our day. It was originally used to identify a behavior during World War II within the context of soldiers' compliance or non-compliance to military expectations; today it helicopters above our emotional landscape and drops a net over anyone whose word usage and body language are boldly and annoyingly out of synch. An example of this is a husband who answers, "Okay, whatever" when his wife asks whether he is willing to repaint the house, after which he slams doors, sulks and barricades himself in the man cave. Even when it is misused or overused, a label of passive-aggressive is never intended as a compliment, and in severe cases of physical or mental aggressiveness resulting in abuse, people need professional help to unpack the chaos of ambivalent words wrapped in a short fuse.

I can safely assume that we all know at least one person who slides easily into the definition of passive-aggressive, someone whose staccato declarations of compliance barely escape a face taut with contempt, a body folded in on itself.

I plead guilty to occasional assaults of passive-aggressive behavior, relational misdemeanors in which fear of the consequences of honesty prevents me from aligning my words with my emotions. But most of the time, passivity is a rare trait in my equally divided Greek and Irish heritage, a genetic hybrid which usually eliminates passive-anything from my life. I am more often programmed for aggressive with a capital A and slightly annoyed even by what is known as the passive voice in writing. This is a style that allows the subject to have something done to it (and usually shows up unexpectedly at the end of the sentence), rather than the active voice which directs the subject up front as the one to hear, think, do, or feel. (A humorous example of this is the difference between the active voice, "Why did the chicken cross the road?" and the passive voice, "Why was the road crossed by the chicken?") My voice finds what needs doing and does it, and thank you very much.

Passive-aggressive people are often chastised for a lack of verbal honesty, but from where I stand, at least they do not need to attempt the impossible task of reversing their river of words and returning them to the headwaters. Aggressive-aggressive people (my new phrase), on the other hand, are rebuked and sometimes shunned for their blunt or unkind words. However, in the face of injustice or neglect within social systems, hospitals, or insurance companies, aggressive-aggressives are a hot (under the collar) commodity.

Are we witnessing a generation of people who bypass the gridlock of speech interchanges on a self-absorbed detour along the communication highway? E-mails and texts and tweets and blogs are uninhabited words—free floating and unattached to bodies—which eliminate the need to interpret crossed arms, blazing eyes, loudly exhaling puffs of frustration, defeated postures. A marriage proposal is texted without a bent knee, a marriage dissolution without the plea of tears. While it is true that many techno-savvy people unfamiliar with the phrase passive-aggressive are not in danger of misinterpreting the language of eyes and arms and hands, it is equally true that these people are unable to engage in multidimensional conversation. How would someone navigate a face-to-face job interview whose only road map has been screen-to-screen monologues?

Although not everyone is knowledgeable of, or interested in the pop-psychology of passive-aggressive, we seem to have staked our territory and divided the phrase into passive and aggressive camps, clearly separating them to protect each from the other. It has become a battle with no hope of peaceful co-existence. Passive people are disdained as the weaker species armed only with killer kindness, unfit to overcome the equally disdained aggressive meat eaters, survivors in the communication jungle fitted with lethal words.

There must be a way for us to savor the texture and variety of personality traits latent in both passive and aggressive people. Many years ago I heard a statement related to marriage that could stretch to cover this issue: If two people are alike, one of them is unnecessary. Why are we so quick to settle for a bland diet of dullness when we could feast on the potluck of peculiarities, the dessert of divine idiosyncrasies? We simply need to reconnect the words passive and aggressive, then uninstall the passive-aggressive program from our hard drive and download a new one. Passive can be defined as humble, amenable, accommodating, settled. Aggressive can be defined as energetic, enterprising, dynamic, code red. With the application of these new descriptions we create a species of humble-energetic, amenable-enterprising, accommodating-dynamic, settled-code red people. What delightful, I-can-live-with-that alternatives to passive-aggressive.

PRAYER AND PLYWOOD

※

I have visited Quebec and Montreal and straddled the California-Mexico border at Rosarita in Baja, but I have never traveled further into Mexico, or at all to Alaska or Hawaii, to Europe or Central America. If I ever get the opportunity to take a vacation or mission trip to any of those places, my checklist will include dazzling sunsets over a lake or ocean, bike rides on picturesque trails, the majesty of multi-hued skies and skin colors and a spirit-quenching variety of languages and cultures.

I could be arm-twisted into traveling to Cancun, the gold standard for resort vacations on the Yucatán peninsula of Mexico. The feet-burning white beaches, azure water, aqua sky, laid-back palm trees, emerald grass and run-on sunshine would be a perfect fit for all of us winter-wearied, freeze-dried Minnesotans. Even a summer pilgrimage to Cancun would earn the silver medal for expansive adventure.

One of John Lennon's famous lyrics is, "Life is what happens to you when you are busy making other plans." Friends of mine who rarely take vacations were in Cancun in August, 2007, happily and uncharacteristically oblivious to all things current. When Don and Chris ambled into the nearest town for basic supplies, they saw people out of tropical synch and overheard discordant sound bites about wind and water and boarding up windows and where would everyone go and what could they carry with them? This was my friends' introduction to Hurricane Dean and their abrupt initiation into the protocol of the evacuation of twenty thousand people.

In the eye of the chaos was a shopkeeper in possession of an eerie calm. "How do you prepare for a hurricane?" Don asked the strangely subdued man. His sanguine reply: "We pray. And we put up a little plywood."

I do not know whether the Cancun shopkeeper took refuge in his boarded-up building or did a hammer-and-flee maneuver, but what is significant is that he prayed *before* he pounded. Prayer becomes both a conscious choice for committed believers and an involuntary reflex for casual Christians and even the spiritually ambivalent. And often prayer downloads a comforting saying, presumably in the Bible, that brings balance during a time of high-wire crisis.

There are many sayings which have, over time, taken on the status of gospel truth. "When God closes a door He always opens a window." (I am guessing the shopkeeper was not thrilled about this promise for his hurricane-proof building.) Another is, "God works in mysterious ways, His wonders to perform." And finally, "God will never give us more than we can handle." These beliefs are defibrillators for hearts beating out of rhythm, pacemakers that become peacemakers. Each sentiment contains big and glorious thoughts ... kind thoughts ... but they are simply not implanted in God's Word.

"When God closes a door He always opens a window," was a line spoken by Maria von Trapp in "The

Sound of Music." "God works in mysterious ways, His wonders to perform," is a marvelous description of an incomprehensible God which appears as the first line of a poem written by William Cowper in 1774.

Perhaps the most widely quoted non-Bible verse is, "God will never give us more than we can handle." The notion that God voluntarily limits what He brings or allows into our lives based on our handling threshold is a loose paraphrase of I Corinthians 10:13. The verse literally reads: "No temptation has overtaken you but such as is common to man; and God is faithful, who will not allow you to be tempted beyond what you are able, but with the temptation will provide the way of escape also, so that you will be able to endure it" (NAS). The apostle Paul wrote these words of assurance to a group of new believers in the city of Corinth who were recent escapees from a prison of sexual immorality and idolatry. The crisis-driven paraphrase becomes something like this: God is faithful and therefore will not allow you to face anything beyond what you are able, without providing a way of escape and a way for you to endure. The actual verse has been retrofitted into a promise about how much God allows in proportion to how much we can handle. It is a sweet, comforting, unscriptural sentiment.

We ride the rapids of life in a raft battered by the raging waters of job loss, family estrangement, bankruptcy, addictions, cancer, the birth of a severely handicapped child, the sudden death of a beloved spouse. When the oars have been ripped from our blistered hands and we are plunging into the death of our plans and dreams, we jettison our cargo of what we can handle. God finally has us where we need Him.

The Old and New Testaments are filled with stories of people who came to the end of themselves: Job,

Moses, Daniel, Queen Esther, Peter, Lazarus. These were people overtaken by destitution, boils, fire, anger, murder, grumblings, threats, even death—all situations that required more hands than they had.

Suppose God chose never to allow more than we could rationalize, understand, fix, solve, eliminate, endure or afford. What would exercise our faith muscles? What would be the purpose of trusting God? As long as we could handle everything tossed into our lives, like street performers juggling flaming swords, we would ultimately man-handle God into a compressed, self-contained space no larger than the size of our strength, a shrink-wrapped God.

Throughout fourteen hundred years of faith history from Genesis to Revelation, God does not reveal Himself as One who limits what He either allows or actively brings in to the lives of His people based on what they can handle. He is a present-tense God Who uses every circumstance to subdue, reduce, conquer and even crush resources, patiently waiting for us to slip through our own fingers and reach for His mighty arms.

When we are convinced that God will never allow more than we can handle, we get busy and start handling. The Cancun shopkeeper finished praying and then put up a little plywood. He made sure God knew he was serious about being part of the solution to the problem he faced. Once God saw him efficiently handling his problem, would He not reward the man's diligence with a takeover operation? This is a clear demonstration of our conviction that "God helps those who help themselves," surely another biblical promise.

This belief, a subtle hybrid of culture and gospel, is satisfying to those of us who are heirs of the Puritan Work Ethic, but this promise does not exist in Scripture.

"God helps those who help themselves" first appeared in 1698 in an article entitled *Discourses Concerning Government* by Algernon Sidney. The axiom literally reads, "God helps him who helps himself," and is more commonly attributed to Benjamin Franklin's *Poor Richard's Almanac* for 1733. It is sound, mature thinking filled with brilliance and sensibility, but God's Word actually proclaims an opposing truth. Romans 5:6 states that "While we were still helpless, at the right time Christ died for the ungodly." Although this refers to our salvation from sin, the principle appears throughout Scripture: When we confess our helplessness, God asks us to move out of His way while He works a plan that does not exist on our radar. Self-reliance, so valued and rewarded in our culture, is a dangerous roadblock to our ability to trust God completely in our lives. This is counter intuitive even in the Christian community that assumes God expects us to time-share our crises with Him in the same way that parents, teachers and employers expect their children, students and employees to invest time and energy into a dilemma before seeking help. "What have you done so far?" is the question that precedes any input from the person in charge. Initiative is rewarded. Lack of effort is discouraged. People who do not try to help themselves out of bad situations and into healthy ones do not earn our respect or receive more than a limited amount of our conditional help. We take pride in being first-responders who arrive at the scene with our physical and mental and emotional equipment pumped and primed. We are dis-inclined to give space or grace to those who bemoan their fate and expect God to drop blessings atop their crossed arms or into pockets crammed with tightly-closed fists.

Deuteronomy chapter eight records all of the gracious and undeserved dealings that God has with His people, none of which they work for or earn. Near the end of the chapter are these words: "In the wilderness He fed you manna which your fathers did not know, that He might humble you and that He might test you, to do good for you in the end. Otherwise, you may say in your heart, 'My power and the strength of my hand made me this wealth'" (NAS).

Our attempts to help may actually be like a firefighter connecting a garden hose to a hydrant: Well-intentioned, proud, full of integrity, but hopelessly inadequate to save a burning building. Our best efforts will never be enough to secure victory.

Does God really want us to tie our hands, bind our abilities, strap down our training? Isn't it recklessly irresponsible to do nothing? How can our idleness bring glory to the same God Who blessed Adam with the gift of creative work?

II Chronicles 20 records the story of King Jehoshaphat facing battle with the sons of Moab and Ammon, a great multitude of warriors. Fearing for his life and the lives of his people, Jehoshaphat turns to the Lord, proclaims a fast, reminds God of everything He has done for the people, and receives this word from the prophet Jahaziel: "You need not fight in this battle; station yourselves, stand and see the salvation of the Lord on your behalf" (NAS).

Imagine the potential humiliation and anger and scorn awaiting a king who refuses to fight; yet that is exactly what is recorded for us in this story. On the day of battle, the king and his people sing and praise and give thanks to God while the Lord busies Himself setting the sons of Moab and Ammon against each other in ambush. When it is time for Jehoshaphat and his people to enjoy the spoils, it takes them three days to carry away everything of value. This is more than a one-for-one reversal of fortunes; it is grandiose, unfathomable abundance poured out on people willing to obey a king who has allowed God to reduce his resources, power and reputation. King Jehoshaphat recites God's blessings, casts away fear, stands still, praises God, holds his ground and waits for God's victory. God, in turn, does not withhold His might until the king and his subjects demonstrate good battle technique; rather, He looks for a heaped up pile of discarded weapons before unleashing His strength.

Although we cannot easily relate to the details of an ancient near-eastern battle story written in the fifth century B.C., there is a universal default setting in crisis mode for all people in all times: Fight. Advocate. Debate. Build. Buy. Sell. Advance. Retreat. Work. We are hard-wired to fight for justice and territory and security, circumstantial evidence that shows we share spiritual genes with our battling ancestors.

Not every war recorded in the Bible is like the one in II Chronicles fought with empty hands, or similar to the one described in Judges 7 in which Gideon's army of 300 men bearing the nonsensical weapons of trumpets, pitchers and torches faces 135,000 armed Midianites. But if God asks us to relinquish our strength, our abilities, our jobs, our homes, our reputations—to empty our hands so that He can gain the upper hand—are we willing?

REST ASSURED

"What is without periods of rest will not endure." Ovid

My grandparents lived and died within a twenty-mile radius of their birthplace. Theirs was not an idyllic, pastoral, Hallmark-movie, good-old-days life. In the late 1920's they were one-room-shack, Mississippi-river-bottom sharecroppers who lost their first-born son at seventeen months of age to a simple intestinal ailment probably caused by poor nutrition. They also lost their second child and eventually raised seven children. By the time I entered the family they lived in a large house in town with electricity, indoor plumbing—all of the things that were an expected part of my childhood.

I did not understand the hard work that framed my grandparents' lives until I was a teenager, and then I did not appreciate it. When I visited them in Ripley, Tennessee during sweltering summers and had the audacity to sleep in until ten o'clock, I was often greeted with "Goooood afternoon!" in the long drawl of my muscular, no-nonsense grandfather as he returned from working his fields, soaked in sweat and looking for "dinner" (which I had to translate as lunch in my Midwestern dialect). Grandma also worked the fields, cooked and canned for a large family—even after all of her children had left home—washed, scrubbed, quilted, and headed to bed before the sun slipped below the horizon. (This was an offense to my night-owlness, since I was also expected to end my day at eight o'clock and awaken to a haughty rooster crowing long before dawn had rubbed the sleep out of its eyes.)

These same grandparents entered rest as heartily as work. Grandpa remained at home while Grandma and I attended Sunday morning church; but each of us embraced a different rhythm on Sundays, a slowing down of responsibility and expectation. Clearly much of this was inevitable from the restrictions enforced by the numerous blue laws passed by many southern states in the mid- to late-1800's to protect Sunday Sabbath. Most of these laws made it illegal for grocery stores and other retail establishments to be open on Sundays. Liquor stores could be open but not make a sale, nor could car dealerships. There are still many blue laws on the books today: In Minnesota it is illegal to purchase alcohol on Sundays, or to purchase a car, although car dealerships can be open. North Dakota has the strictest remaining blue laws still in existence in the United States: All retail stores must be closed from midnight Saturday until two o'clock Sunday afternoon, although a 1991 blizzard relaxed some of the laws, enabling people to purchase necessary goods and services on Sunday morning.

It could certainly be argued that laws which require mandatory Sabbath observance do not change hearts with any greater success than the other ten commandments. There is, however, a frightening ease with which our goal-oriented church culture skims over the command to rest as though it were a parenthetical remark, a grammatical, last-minute add-on, an afterthought to God's completed work rather than a deliberate creation.

"Then God blessed the seventh day and sanctified it, because in it He rested from all His work which God created and made" (Genesis 2:2-3, NAS). The commandment to honor the Sabbath is number four, the hinge between the first four commandments which govern our relationship with God and the last six which guide our relationships with people. A healthy obedience to honor the gift of Sabbath expands, clarifies and guards both relationships.

When we identify the Sabbath and then set it apart, we actually set ourselves aside and restore God as the center of our lives, something which needs doing again and again. Exhaled breath and dropped shoulders give us time and space to look back, around and forward; to see what God *has* done, *is* doing and *will* do in our lives: three verb tenses that reflect the Trinity-Authority of Sabbath rest.

Sabbath is the exclamation point of God's work, the recognition of unhurried perfection. It is both the first and last thing He proclaims as a Holy gift. "And I heard a voice from heaven, saying, 'Write, 'Blessed are the dead who die in the Lord from now on!' 'Yes,' says the Spirit, 'so that they may rest from their labors, for their deeds follow with them'" (Revelation 14:13, NAS). Thus, from Genesis to Revelation, God uses Sabbath as bookends for His Word and as a whole-note rest in the music of His World. (David wrote a Psalm which contains the lyric, "Return to your rest, O my soul.")

Sabbath rest is the punctuation necessary to prevent run-on lives and align our interactions with people. (Jesus said, "Come to me all you who are weary and heavy-laden, and I will give you rest.") God's rest is not the late-night, semi-comatose repetition of a 1950's TV test pattern; it is a high-resolution search light seeking His best above everything that is merely better, a wide-angle view of our lives through the lens of Godly gain, not just good and plenty activity. We can scatter ourselves out across the vast horizon of work, but the call is not always embedded in the need. Our raw gifts and recognized abilities are not an automatic green light for teaching Sunday School, mowing the church lawn, contributing time and money to fund-raisers, petitions, mission trips, soup kitchens, nursing homes, committees, school projects and community functions. Just as God's Word tells us to guard our minds, hearts and lips, it also encourages us to guard our time. (Moses wrote in Psalm 90, "Teach us to number our days, that we may present to You a heart of wisdom.") If we do not step out of our daily shoes and bury our feet in God's Sabbath-soil we may wear through our soles doing good works, praise-worthy works that are not part of God's plan for either our character development or His Kingdom building. Conversely, if we agree to a work that does not ignite our passion simply because we feel obligated to do it, or no one else will do it, or someone will be angry or disappointed in us if we fail to do it, we will likely wear through our souls.

God created Sabbath-wrapped, vibrant rest. Our only responsibility is to hold it with respectful, holy hands. Why is that so difficult? When we fill our Sabbath cup with work and then try to top if off with rest, the rest is the first to spill onto ground trampled by overwhelmed, under-joyed feet. Why do we resist God's gift? Are we afraid that if we stop too suddenly, we will cramp our productivity muscles?

Sabbath rest is not a failsafe protection against crises and heartaches, but it deadbolts our spirit against rest robbers—in my case, anxiety over what I cannot control. It also insulates us from frenetic and useless activity, much like trying to pedal a bike

careening downhill. Even useful activity requires downtime, allowing ourselves to be regularly benched the way volleyball players and bowling pins are rotated out of the game.
    Sabbath rest cannot be exhausted.
    Sabbath rest is commanded renewal.
    God has given us Sabbath rest. Assured.

SIZING IT UP

It looks like an enormous, concrete-coated spaceship with a sky blue dome and elaborate half-moon portal windows surrounding the top. Inside are balconies, golden spiral staircases, blue leather seats, ornate crosses hiding air conditioning vents; brass, icons, gates, stained glass glory. It is the Annunciation Greek Orthodox Church in Milwaukee, Wisconsin, designed by Frank Lloyd Wright in 1951. It is arguably one of the most easily recognizable buildings in the state and was my childhood church for two years, along with visitation rights over the next several years for weddings and funerals.

I do not remember the size of the Annunciation Greek Church congregation, one which pre-dated the "new" building by fifty years. The multi-layered floor and balcony seating will hold one thousand, but any amount of people would be dwarfed by the height, the circumference, the sheer volume of space within this circular cathedral.

In profound contrast to this church is a part brick, part aluminum-sided building housing a utilitarian sanctuary with tiled floors, wooden pews and one wooden cross behind the pulpit. Brown Deer Baptist Church in Brown Deer, Wisconsin—the next leg of my spiritual journey— is an unassuming Southern Baptist Church hundreds of miles north of the Mason-Dixon Line and home to about one hundred people, a congregation that fits easily in the hip pocket of the denomination.

From fourth grade through high school, I nestled securely in the arms of a church family noticeably different than my biological one: It was a well-oiled, appropriately filled, happily working unit that never tried to run on emotional fumes. I quickly and gratefully embraced this group of grace-centered, extravagant encouragers—master-degreed dispensers of patience and love—even as they encircled me. Moreover, lives do not come in self-cleaning models, even for children, and they were also clay-footed saints who led me to Jesus for a gentle but thorough scouring of my messes, scrubbing of my resentments, cleansing of my failures, and washing of my heart.

During my teen years, my economy-sized youth group shared the universal desire of Christian teens: To flow into a larger river of singing, studying, playing, praying, growing, and trolling (for a spouse). There were several different places outside of my church that met our needs: before-school Bible Studies, Saturday night coffee houses, concerts, lock-ins, camp-outs and Sunday evening services at large churches that necessitated the eventual inclusion of megachurch in the Protestant lexicon.

I still enjoy attending retreats and conferences, and visiting substantial churches with my family when my pastor husband is on vacation, but my adult experience has been in churches similar in size and function to my childhood Baptist church. I have switched denominations to one which has over 830 churches in the United States and Canada alone, the majority of which number fewer than one hundred people. I do not know the statistics regarding the demographics and careers and overall makeup of the congregations in those churches, but I know that my present church is a gift of people who are giants of prayer, committed to connection and spiritual growth, and who share the joy of belonging with those who might otherwise worship in obscurity, camouflaged in the landscape of churches more populous than many towns.

In the forty years since my teenage introduction to a megachurch, there has been a flood of books and movements addressing the necessity and desirability of numerical church growth modeled by the earliest church as recorded in the book of Acts, in which, "The Lord was adding to their number day by day those who were being saved". When I typed the words "church growth" into my computer search engine I found 890 websites addressing this ecclesiastical hot topic, and 810 websites addressing "megachurch." A turbo-charged church that can go from fifteen to fifteen hundred people in four-point-three years is a guaranteed success story. This is ironic in light of the following incredible statistic taken from the Saguaro Buttes Community Church website: "Small churches of less than one hundred people make up 59% (177,000) of the 300,000 congregations in the USA." There are many instances of vital New Testament congregations which met in homes like that of Priscilla and Aquilla, also chronicled in the book of Acts. There was endless variety in the fledgling New Testament church, with a diversity of sizes as well as personalities and hot-button issues eternally relevant. But in our bigger-is-better, more-is-best culture we are easily hypnotized by swinging words like megabuck, megabyte, megahertz, megawatt, supercharged, superconductor, superglue, supermodel, superhighway, supernova, supersize.

We are drawn to the raging bonfire of a megachurch. A candle-watt congregation often apologizes for its modest flame.

Do we see small home church or public church congregations as weaker versions of larger churches in which muscle is measured by the circumference of numerical growth and the strength of programming prowess? Our heavenly Father likely weighs any size church by the maturity of its body, the strength of its hands to rightly handle the Word of Truth, and the support of its four-walled neighborhood where people cross theological fences to synchronize their lives. The illnesses of toddlers, fits and starts of teenagedom, issues of aging and fear of financial insecurity all become watch alarms awakening us to share meals and laughter, tears and prayers, celebrations and quiet vigils, the spiritual rhythm of life and death and life again. The slim-size church shares equal privileges and responsibilities with the huskier body of Christ. In God's more-or-less kingdom, less is more: A lean body can experience big growth measured by the connective tissue of forgiveness and the tendons of joy.

WHEN ALL ELSE FAILS II

When the safety net unravels under the tightrope;
when we dangle over the cliff of understanding;
when pale-knuckled fingers lose their grip;
when a closed door leads to a jammed window;
when the cabin loses pressure;
when resources are compressed into tight spaces;
when the water seeps out of a half-empty glass;
when all else has failed, we pray.
The battle of knockdown, drag-out faith begins.
God is exactly where we left Him.
When we fix our eyes on Jesus instead of the sagging rope;
when we cling to the lone Tree of Life and resist the urge to look down;
when we open our hands and grab the Nail-scarred One;
when we find the Door of Life;
when we place the Spirit's mask over our mouths and inhale life-giving Breath;
when we discover an abundant storehouse;
when we drink from the everlasting wellspring;
when all else has paled, we rejoice.
The battle belongs to the Lord.
God is exactly where we found Him.

SPARE PARTS

I have an extensive collection of fiction, biographies, non-fiction, Caldecott- and Newberry-Award winning children's literature and classic novels which grace six large oak bookshelves and lend dignity to our home. Yes, they are old-fashioned books which are like my friends, to be experienced and enjoyed countless times. I sometimes wonder if, apart from the pure satisfaction of the words washing over my spirit, I revisit my books hoping to either change the ending (maybe this time Rhett Butler will be convinced of Scarlett O'Hara's genuine love) or complete subplots which never cross the finish line (perhaps Atticus Finch will seek justice for the abused and pathetic Mayella Ewell).

Although Jesus' parables are brilliant one-act plays, my mind still works in full-length feature film mode and longs to draw out the stories. What happened to the older brother in the parable of the Prodigal Son? Did he help slaughter the fatted calf, attend the feast, dance and cut loose? Did he accept God's insulating grace as heart-protection against the chill of envy? Did he rejoice in the gift of obedience? Or did he become an emotional prodigal separated from his family by miles of resentment?

Why is the narrative of Job completely silent about his wife after chapter two? If she suffered as much loss as Job, did she rejoice in a second chance at a home and family?

Were Pilate's inadequately washed hands ever cleansed by the Risen Christ?

Did the beaten man in the parable of the Good Samaritan resent the care he received from his despised enemy? Did he try to repay the Samaritan so that he could be released from any debt of gratitude? Or did the greatest healing occur in his heart?

Basic Parenting 101 has clear guidelines for children whose errant feet get caught in the net of lies: They must walk a probationary path back toward trust. This is the same journey for damaged employer-employee relationships. And yet this was not at all how Jesus treated Peter after his triple denial. Jesus did not say, "Peter, go home to your family, think about what you did, and return to me (if I'm still here) after a sufficient amount of time has passed to convince me that you are truly remorseful." The Bible does not paint this word picture. I assume that Peter did not have to earn Jesus' trust since He saw ahead to the bold faith Peter would show for the rest of his life. But even without that ability to see the future, maybe time-bound parents should consider looking for ways to restore our children to immediate usefulness in our families, just as Jesus restored Peter to instant and significant work in the Kingdom.

The book of Proverbs praises both the wisdom of a few counselors and the wisdom of an abundance of them. How do we know when we need a few good men or women, and when we need a troop to advise us?

The same God Who did not give Adam and Eve a second chance before banishing them from the Garden gave Moses multiple chances before forbidding him entry to the Promised Land. Who can understand His ways? He is God. We are not. Thank God.

Sometimes we turn the other cheek. Other times we seek justice to save the face of someone who has been robbed of value.

I live in northern Minnesota. While some people wonder whether March will come in like a lamb and go out like a lion, or come in like a lion and go out like a lamb, my energy and emotions converge at the focal point of grit and stamina required to endure two more fifty-day months (or so it seems) of winter when the meteorological calendar proclaims spring. Sometimes we are treated to "thunder snow," an awesome and rare event around Lake Superior which, if it occurs in late March, provides a wet, weighty layer of jumbo flakes to cover the black, crusty piles of decomposed snow lining the sides of the roads. When spring finally emerges from its elongated hibernation, I always hope it will not decide to pull a blanket of post-winter detritus over its head and return to an extended slumber.

The lamb-lion March saying does not affect or reflect Minnesota climate, but it is a picture of Jesus, Who entered the world as the Passover Lamb and will return as the Lion of Judah. The Word of God marches on. Hallelujah.

What does it really mean to give someone "the benefit of the doubt," or to trust someone "beyond the shadow of a doubt?" Apparently doubts have both benefits and shadows, which is confusing and a bit mind-bending. I do not know if I am capable of understanding the shadow, but I can break down the benefit part. A benefit is an advantage; a doubt is an undecided state of mind. In the benefit of the doubt the advantage tips in favor of the person whose past has exhibited trustworthy behavior.

Enter Doubting Thomas, the most famous or infamous doubter in history. Through him we see greater benefits to doubt than we could ever imagine. Thomas' doubt allows him to touch Jesus, who in turn shows Thomas the benefit of the doubt. A bold touch motivated by doubt yields an advantage of profound faith.

It seems that a favorite pastime for Believers is pinpointing all of the dark corners of our world, places where sin is sullen, ominous, pitch black, jet black, the blackest of black. We are certain that our generation has exposed sin that is darker and more twisted than any the world has seen. Humankind is teetering on a precipice, ready to implode into the depth of its own sinfulness, a sure sign that Jesus is ready to return to earth.

Have Christians become defined by what we despise? Known by our negativism? Remembered for our reactionary behavior? We should never blur the lines of sin, but there is nowhere in Scripture that calls us to be drum majors in the parade of darkness proclamation. Our finite time spent cursing the darkness is a hammer endlessly and futilely pounding on the same nail without completing even one building in God's earthly kingdom. In divine contrast, Jesus called Himself the Light of the World and commanded us to reflect His Light, to be a bright city on a hill and to uncover His Shining Glory. We do not need to hold the darkness under water hoping to drown it while fearing its power. Light abides in quiet confidence while darkness flees.

Every child stands on the threshold of adulthood with the words, "*You* will pay for what you did!" reverberating through his memory chamber. Children break windows and toys and bones and glasses and trust. Reversal of damage carries a price tag. Responsible parents teach their children to pay that price, usually with an age-appropriate amount of money or work. When restitution is made, the hope is that the children will be richer in maturity.

Every person stands on the threshold of eternity with Jesus' words, "*I* will pay for what you did!" reverberating through the very Word. People break laws and hearts, sinfulness that severs the intended relationship between man and God. Reversal of the damage of sin carries only one price tag—death—but Jesus covers the cost. As the responsible party, Jesus teaches that money and work are not valid currency and restitution in heaven. People are offered the ultimate gift—grace that makes no cents—and with that grace, they walk into the Kingdom with an extravagance of wealth.

I once heard that the Church is the only organization that shoots its fallen. Christians deeply embedded in the

Church may have lost the ability to spot the Real Enemy. Career foot soldiers supposedly fighting on the side of righteousness wear deep scars from friendly fire. We who have good intentions of guarding Truth carry grenades packed with accusation and carefully lob them across an expanse separating factions within the camp of believers—factions held together by a common cord of age, gender, race, personality, political affiliation, end-times theology and social justice issues. These hard-won factions live within barbed-wire-enclosed Truth. Free-range armored tanks filled with high-octane legalism occasionally cross the demilitarized zone and crush the injured struggling for a last gasp of grace.

Philip Yancey, one of my favorite authors and theologians, has shared his childhood experience of attending a Bible belt church in the 1960's, a church which gradually tightened its buckle until there was no chance to catch even a shallow breath of freedom in Christ. Thankfully he has healed from those wounds, but he uses his experience of Post-Traumatic Enemy Confusion to enlist the disillusioned and disenfranchised for a tour of a grace-paved trail to the Savior.

Let us read the advance intelligence reports in the Word of God to identify our guerrilla warfare-trained Enemy: The Destroyer. The Double Agent. The Liar. The Deceiver. The Accuser. The Discourager. The Enemy may try to hide behind our brothers and sisters in the family of God, but we must expose and ambush him until all his supply lines are cut off.

I have not always felt welcome in the twenty-first technocentury. While I am extremely grateful for the ease of writing afforded by my computer, it seems that general language skills—always considered essential for social interaction—have had a head-on collision with computers and other screens-of-choice. The resulting debris has littered our communication freeway with the encrypted messages of e-mail, facebook, texting and tweeting. My eyes are assaulted by partial phrases and dangling consonants that could never measure up to the Gettysburg Address or Hamlet's Soliloquy.

I will admit that I was swept up in Instant Messaging (quietly decaying under strata of newer technologies). It was incredibly satisfying to be able to "talk" to friends in this new way. When IMing was all the rage, I thought about how the Bible was way ahead of its time in computerese. The book of Exodus records God asking Moses to go before Pharaoh; when Moses responds, "Whom should I say sent me?" God replies, "Say that I AM sent you." The book of John records the seven I AM statements of Jesus: "I AM the Bread of Life; I AM the Light of the World; I AM the Door; I AM the Good Shepherd; I AM the Resurrection and the Life; I AM the Way, the Truth and the Life; I AM the True Vine."

God the I Am and His Living Word are the Ultimate IM.

We recently observed the tenth anniversary of the 9/11 attacks on our country. There are two prevalent theories which gain greater traction each year: 9/11

was our own government's conspiracy, which in turn empowers Homeland Security and an untold number of agencies to gradually choke us until we drop all of our rights; or, it was clearly an extreme Muslim conspiracy which continues to justify all of our military involvements in the Middle East. Portions of these theories combine in hybrids of fear and trust and disdain and uncertainty.

I meet many people who find it easier and more oddly comforting to believe that the assumed good guys with the white hats—our own government—sold us down the river, than to believe that the bad guys—whomever they may be—were capable of the unfathomable horror of 9/11. Why is this so? How is evil hiding behind good more palatable than evil begging to be identified? And why is a conspiracy of evil more compelling than the lone variety? History's most infamous wickedness was not tied to a conspiracy, but was instead associated with one person recognized by one name: Nero. Hitler. Stalin.

As I scrolled through my facebook postings on 9/11 I discovered the following mini-dialogue: "Question: Sir, what is wrong with this world? Answer: I am. What is wrong with the world is inside of me." There will always be conspiracy theories about every country-altering event from the Kennedy assassination to 9/11. The thread that ties all of the disparate opinions together is the quiet truth that the darkest darkness resides in each of us, and it is only God's mercy that can restore us and give us dignity.

Those of us who place our hope in God are freed from the need to either attack or defend our government or any other. Governments and agencies and communities and laws are temporal. God's Kingdom is built one changed heart at a time; that alone is our security and our peace.

My mother was one of a generation of women who believed the saying, "Cleanliness is next to godliness." She took it as gospel truth. Walls and floors and pots and pans were scrubbed and polished and sanitized to within an inch of their natural lives.

Turns out that ours is a different gospel: "Godliness is next to uncleanliness." Jesus-the-man became ritually unclean and gained the scorn of the Pharisees every time he walked among the defiled: Gentiles, Samaritans, tax collectors, lepers. Jesus-the-God power-washed their hearts until they were cleaned for eternity.

PART III

THROUGH YOUR OWN REARVIEW MIRROR

COMPLETE SIGNAL LOSS

AN EMPTY TOMB AND A FULL NET

CATCH AND RELEASE MARRIAGE

CROSS PURPOSES:
A GRAVE INTENT

FULL HOUSE: THE MOUNT OF TRANSFIGURATION

MANNA: NO REFRIGERATION REQUIRED

OFF THE GRID

ROUGH DRAFT

UNDER CONSTRUCTION

PLAY UNTIL THE WHISTLE BLOWS